THE TAMILIAN ANTIQUARY

THE TAMILIAN ANTIQUARY

EDITOR
PANDIT D. SAVARIROYAN
VOL. I, NO. I-10; VOL. II, NO. 1-2
VOL. II. NO. 1

AN OLD TRADITION PRESERVED
V.J. TAMBY PILLAI
A NOTE ON THE SANGAM PERIODS
D. SAVARIROYAN
THE ANTIQUITY OF NANJINAD
AND SHENKOTTAH
THE TWO TAMIL DISTRICTS OF TRAVANCORE
T. PONNAMBALAM PILLAI
SAGE PAVANANDHI, CRITIC AND TEACHER
M.S. PURNALINGAM PILLAI
DRAVIDIAN COINS
T.M. RENGACHARIAR & T. DESIKACHARIAR
THE KURAL
REV. J. LAZARUS
A CHAPTER FROM THE KURAL
J.M. NALLASWAMI PILLAI
THE TAMILS IN THE EPIC AGE
M. RAGHAVA AIYANGAR
LANKA AND THE TAMIL SANGAMS
A. MUTUTTHAMBY PILLAI
PANDIYAN COINS
T. DESIKACHARIAR

4 PLATES

GYAN

Published by

Gyan Publishing House
5, Ansari Road
Daryaganj, New Delhi-110002
Phone: 011-47034999, 9811692060
E-mail: books@gyanbooks.com

Distribution Network
gyanbooks.com
India, USA, Canada, UK, Australia, France

ISBN : 978-81-212-4493-0 (HB)
First Published, 1913

2nd Impression 2020

Printed at: Gyan Press, Delhi.

An Old Tradition Preserved.

BY

MR. V. J. TAMBY PILLAI, M.R.A.S.

THERE were many wonders in the world, they say, such as the pyramids of Egypt, the leaning tower of Pisa, the floating islands of Mexico and the hanging gardens of Babylon. As monuments of human skill and ingenuity, perseverance and energy in the field of architecture, they have always occupied a foremost place in the estimation of civilized man. There are, however, other wonders amongst us equally, if not more wonderful than these, in other fields which have yet to be explored, appreciated and admired. India has been considered the land of wonders. Its literature is the oldest in the world and its philosophy the most profound in more respects than one. The problems it presents in the field of philology are still more wonderful, embracing, as they do, a field as large as a hundred languages and dialects, yet divided only into two great distinct and separate families called the Southern and the Northern or the Tamilian and the Aryan languages. Of these two great linguistic monuments, by far the most wonderful by its antiquity and vitality is the first, *viz.* the most highly developed and richest of all the languages of the Dravidas, I mean the Tamil. Empires have risen and fallen, the boundaries of countries have changed, and new nations and religions have sprung up, flourished and decayed since this wonder of the old country of Bharata was evolved. An old tradition that has been preserved to our day in some of the classical works in this language locates the beginning of its cultivation in the hoary past, far beyond the times when the ancestors of the primitive Aryans set foot on the frontiers of the Punjab, nay, when the Cimmerian nomads were wandering after their flocks and herds in the highlands of

Central Asia. The tradition asserts that South India was the seat of a powerful dynasty for many centuries from a very remote time and that the capital of the dynasty was the seat of an assembly of learned men, which continued to flourish throughout three successive periods separated from one another by two deluges, one universal and the other partial.

These assemblies of *literati* were, hence, known as the first, second, and third Sangams, of which the first flourished at the Southern Madura for a period of 4400 years and comprised of about 4449 authors. The names of some of them have also been preserved and they are Agastiyar (அகத்தியர்), Siva (சிவன்) or Thiripurameritta Virisadi Kadavul (திரிபுரமெரித்த விரிசடைக்கடவுள்), Murinchiyur Mudinagar (முரிஞ்சியூர் முடிநாகர்) or Adisedan (ஆதிசேடன்), Kuperan (குபேரன்) or Irunitikkilavan (இருநிதிக்கிழவன்), Subramanyar (சுப்பிரமணியர்) or Kunram Erinta Murugavel (குன்றமெறிந்த முருகவேள்), Vanmikiyar (வான்மீகையார்), Markandeyar (மார்க்கண்டேயர்) etc. According to the tradition, the num[illegible] Pandiyans who maintained this S[illegible]gam is 89 from Kaysinav[illegible]uty (காய்சினவழுதி) to Kadunkon (கடுங்கோன்), of whom seven were themselves great authors. A huge deluge which submerged a vast extent of land extending from Cape Comorin southwards—so says the tradition—closed the first period of Tamil literature, all the literary productions of the time having been washed away by the waters, and the Pandiyan, his nobles and people being destroyed at the same time. Of the works composed during this period, the names of a few have been preserved and they are Agattiyam (அகத்தியம்) Isainunukkam (இசைநுணுக்கம்) Kuruku (குருகு), Narai (நாரை) etc.

The second period of the Tamil *literature* lasted according to the tradition during the reigns of 59 Pandiyans from Pandiyan Vendercheliyan (வெண்டேர்ச் செழியன்) to Pandiyan Mudathirumaran (முடத்திருமாறன்), five of whom were themselves poets; and covered a period of 3700 years. It sat at the 2nd Capital of the Pandiyans called Kapadapuram (கபாடபுரம்)

by some, and Alaivai (அலைவாய்) by others. A second deluge occurred and destroyed the Capital of the Pandiyan and washed off all the books stored up in the library. The names of a few of the authors who flourished during this period and who numbered 3700 in all, have also been preserved, and these are Agattiyar (அகத்தியர்), Tolkappiyar (தொல்காப்பியர்), Vellurkappiyar (வெள்ளூர்க்காப்பியர்), Kirantaiyar (கீரந்தையர்), Tuvaraikkoman (துவரைக்கோமான்) etc. The names of some important grammatical works which were studied in this period are also known, and they are Tolkappiyam (தொல்காப்பியம்), Agattiyam (அகத்தியம்), Mapuranam (மாபுராணம்), Putapuranam (பூதபுராணம்) etc.; of which Tolkappiyam is still extant, while Agattiyam and Mapuranam would seem to have also been extant till very recent times. The third Sangam sat at the Modern Madura and lasted throughout the reigns of 49 Pandiyans from Mudathirumaran (முடத்திருமாறன்) to Ukkrapperuvaluty (உக்கிரபெருவழுதி); the total length of the period covered by it being about 1850 years. Three of the Pandiyans who maintained the Sangam were also among the assembly of authors who numbered 449 in all, most of whose works were extant till a few centuries ago. The above is a short summary of the tradition concerning the famous Tamil Sangams.

The question now arises whether the above tradition contains any authentic historical facts and, if so, whether it is to be believed in whole or only in part. First of all, I might observe that, in judging of the trustworthiness of the account, one should take into consideration that the members of the Hindu pantheon such as Sivan, Murugan, Kuperan and others were all not gods in reality, but deified celebrities of the olden times; secondly, that even allowing that these celebrities were gods in reality, the historical character of the tradition is by no means impaired by the wrong identification in question, for they can be easily explained as later interpolations. The traditions and legends current in a country can never be said to have originated in the inventive faculties or any evolutionary process going on in the inner consciousness of any individual, however learned or unlearned he may be.

Some years ago, an old man of 90 years, in relating to me the history of the apparition of a comet in his younger days, told me that the comet had a long tail which after sometime broke off in the middle and fell on the earth somewhere in the regions of the west and lay there for several days sending forth a very offensive smell. What degree of credence the latter part of this story demands from us, it is hardly necessary to state. But, however foolish and absurd it may be, its origin would seem easy to account for when it is remembered that the illiterate mind of the vulgar might have found an excuse or reason for formulating the theory in the fact of the comet's tail having appeared shorter and shorter as it soared up into the depths of space towards the western sky. It is indeed a historical fact, that a big comet appeared in the time indicated by the old man as I myself have ascertained on enquiry.

Again, the learned author of the Mahawansa has recorded a tradition prevalent in his time concerning Sinhabahu, the father of the first Sinhalese king of Ceylon, according to which, the father of Sinhabahu was a lion and the name of Sinhabahu was given te the lion's son from the fact of his having inherited the hands and feet of his lion-father. The Mahawansa makes mention also of a maiden named Ḳiveni, the daughter of a Yakka chief of Ceylon, who had three breasts one of which had been predicted to disappear at the sight of him who was destined to become her husband; accordingly on her first meeting with Prince Wijaya soon after the arrival of the latter in Ceylon, her third breast disappeared and the predicted marriage also subsequently came on. We have a similar story in the history of Jaffna concerning two of its ancient Kings, Vîr Ukkirasingan and Narasingan; the history credits the former with a lion's face and the latter with a lion's face and tail. Instances of this kind can be multiplied indefinitely in which even learned writers have been led away by the current of popular opinions and fancies; but no competent scholar has hitherto disputed the historical worth of the other part of the narratives which relate to the fact of the existence of Sinhabahu of Sinhapuram, or the marriage of Prince Wijaya with the Yakka princess Kiveni, or of the reigns of Ukkirasingan and his son Narasingan over the kingdom of Jaffna, although fabulous and mythical accretions have gathered around their names. After all, what at first sight appears to be hopelessly fabulous in the stories given above will, on a closer inspection of the names of the characters, be found to be easily explainable. It has to be noticed that the names Sinhabahu, Ukkirasingan and Narasingan have one part in common, Viz., Singam, just as they were said to possess leonine features; and the origin of the myths in their case is therefore clearly traceable to the important attempt of a light-pated author to give the *raison d' etre* of these names.

If, then, the history of Sinhababu, Wijaya, Ukkirasingan and Narasingan as recorded in the history of Jaffna and Ceylon can be regarded as authentic in the main, notwithstanding the myths and fables which have got mixed up with it, would it not be a gross mistake to reject in *toto* the traditions concerning the Tamil Sangams? If the mere fact that Sivan, the philosopher of the first Sangam, has been identified with the God of the same name, and the poet, Naga King of Murinchiur (முரிஞ்சியூர் முடிநாகர்) with the king of the serpents by a certain fanciful writer, invalidate the historical worth of the whole account of the Sangam, then the three breasts of Kiveni and the leonine features of Sinhabahu, Ukkirasingan and others equally impair the authenticity of the whole of their recorded histories. But this is a conclusion at which no competent scholar has yet arrived. Besides these facts, the opinion entertained by many a western *savant*, viz., that the Gods of the Hindus are merely their deified heroes and sages of antiquity, would appear, in the bsence of any more satisfactory explanations, to afford us a clue to the right understanding of the divine membership of the First Sangam.

One more critical remark which deserves some notice here is that which relates to the respective lengths of the periods of the Sangams. I am ready to admit that the figures given are possibly untrustworthy; but I affirm that this inaccuracy does not necessarily, if at all, lead one to the conclusion that the Sangam did not exist at all. Are we to reject the little because the more has not been given, or, discard the imperfect because the perfect is not available? There is in fact no book or record of sufficient antiquity which is free from textual errors and much less from numerical inaccuracies. Even the Hebrew scriptures which are admitted to be the most historical of all the extant histories of ancient times have not escaped mistakes of this kind.

I now proceed to consider whether and to what extent the tradition can he accepted as containing facts of authentic history. I start, of course, from the premise that tradttions in general always embody in a more or less distorted form actual historical facts which form their core and centre, and which with the aid of information derived from other allied sources can often be gleaned and brought within the pale of authentic history. The main or the central facts of the tradition now before us, on the truth or falsity of which its fate must necessarily depend, are obviously the following, viz., 1. that a large continent once existed in the Indian Ocean which was connected with or contiguous to Southern India and which was overwhelmed and submerged by a huge deluge; 2. that Southern India was the seat of human habitation from very remote times; 3. that the race which occupied it in those primitive times was a highly civilised and an eminently literary one; 4. that it possessed extensive literature, and 5. that Southern India was the seat of a very powerful dynasty for several centuries from the very remotest times till some centuries ago.

The above would seem to represent, briefly, the essence of the whole tradition, on the cred. .ity or otherwise of which, as I have already stated, the fate of the Tamil Sangams depends. First of all we are confronted with the question of a universal or partial deluge which overwhelmed the primitive Dravidians. That such a deluge occurred within the recollections of the primitive races is a fact which no scholar will be disposed to deny. The Hebrew scriptures have preserved a fairly distinct account of an appalling catastrophe of this kind, according to which the deluge was occasioned by continuous heavy showers of rain for 40 days and nights coupled with the overflow of the waters of the Ocean which, Scientists say, was occasioned by the *subsidence of the land.* If the deluge described in the Hebrew records and the deluge mentioned in the tradition of the Dravidians refer to one and the same event, the historical character of the reference to a deluge made in the tradition receives full corroboration and it only remains to be added that whereas the Hebrew records do not give us any definite indications of the particular part of the surface of the globe which was the abode of the anti-diluvian man, the Dravidian tradition gives definite information on this interesting point and locates the anti-diluvian habitation of the Tamilian races, if not of the whole human race, in a large continent which once stood above the waters of the Indian Ocean of which the present Southern India forms a part. "The locality of the origin of the earliest race from the most recent researches appears to have been" says a writer to the *Science of Man*, Australia, for December 1900, "on lands now submerged beneath the Indian Ocean." "The Indian Ocean formed a continent", says Professor Haeckel, "which extended from Sunda Islands along the coast of Asia to the east coast of Africa. This large continent of former times is of great importance from being the probable cradle of the human race." Topinard says that "Geology and Natural History make it alike certain that at a time, within the bounds of human knowledge, Southern India did not form part of Asia.

A large Southern Contintent of which this country once formed part has ever been assumed as necessary to account for the different circumstances. The Ceylon Budhists and the Puranic writers and the local traditions of the west coast all indicate a great disturbance of the point of the Peninsula and Ceylon within recent times." Sir John Evans, in his presidential address at the British Association, 1897, referred to the probability of the Southern India being the cradle of the human race. ("Science of Man", August 1901.) "Investigations in relation to race," says Dr. Maclean in his Manual of the Administration of the Madras Presidency, "show it to be by no means impossible that Southern India was once the passage ground by which the ancient progenitors of Northern and Mediterranean races proceeded to the parts of the globe which they now inhabit. Human remains and traces have been found on the east coast of an age which is indeterminate but quite beyond the ordinary calculations of history. Antiquarian research is only now beginning to find means of supplementing the deficiency caused by the absence of the materials constructed or collected by usual historical methods. These results are espcially to be regretted as, without doubt, the people who have for many ages occupied this portion of the peninsula are a great people influencing the world not much perhaps by moral and intellectual attributes but to a great extent by superior physical qualities."

The above opinions of some of the expert scientists of the day will only leave one impression in the mind of any honest reader. The agreement between them and the South Indian tradition is wonderful and striking. Centuries before the Sciences of Geology and Natural History were born, the records of Southern India had in no uncertain voice declared the fact that once a continent existed in the Indian ocean of which Southern India formed part and that a watery catastrophe overwhelmed the races who occupied the districts to the south of the present Cape Comorin.

I have so far dealt with the question how the Dravidian tradition of a deluge and of the submersion of a vast extent of land under the waters of the Indian ocean is supported by the conclusions of modern science and how ill-founded are the opinions of a few who sought to bring it under the category of worthless myths.

I beg to draw here the attention of the reader to the observations made by the late Prof. Seshagiri Sastriar, M. A., on the subject, which are quite ill-founded and totally untenable. He, in a brochure of his entitled *An Essay on Tamil Literature*, remarks thus: "With reference to the first two Sangams, I may say that the account is too mythical and fabulous to be entitled to any credit and I do not think that any scholar who has studied the histories of the world will be bold enough to admit such tales within the pale of real history. There may have been some truth in the above account as regards the Government of the Madura Kingdom by the Pandiyans, but the number of the kings who are said to have ruled over the Kingdom, viz., 89 Pandiyans who are connected with the first Sangam and 59 who are connected with the intervening Sangam is not quite trustworthy and to accept it as a true fact we require some further evidence." From the above quotation, it is evident that Mr. Seshagiri Sastriar disposed of the whole account of the first and the second Sangams as entirely worthless. It is undoubtedly the extraordinarily long periods of the Pandiyan regime as well as the identification of Siva, the poet, with the God of that name and similar identifications of the other poets with some other members of the Hindu pantheon, which has led him to make such a sweeping statement concerning the first two Sangams; but that he has been hasty in his conclusions and indulged in an incorrect and unscientific survey of the different bearings of the tradition will be apparent as we have shown in the foregoing pages. We should indeed be extremely thankful for at least a few more particulars concerning this awful watery crisis; but the records which might possibly have afforded us this information have all perished, having been swept away by a second flood as the tradition states; or, it may be by the natural wear and tear of ages, the internecine wars of the South Indian princes, the strife for supremacy between rival religious sects, the devastations caused by the Musalman invasion or the ephemeral character of the materials on which books were written, or by all these causes combined. It must be admitted that the extant literature in Tamil represents, in fact, so small a portion of the learning and knowledge which was once locked up in it that we can hardly go through any extant old commentary on any of our classical work without experiencing a sense of utmost pain or heaving an unconscious sigh as the highly polished and classical quotations and names of old standard works on Grammar, Theology, Metaphysics etc., of which there would seem to have been quite an ocean, as it were, in ancient times, pass in review before us and remind us of the ancient grandeur and wealth of *the* first language of Baratakandam and of its present comparative indigence.

In view of these facts it is only reasonable to suppose that the source of the information preserved in the tradition as regards the total number of Pandiyans, *viz.* 196, who reigned during the Sangam periods, was in some of the numerous classical works which once existed in Southern India and that it was from some fragmentary remains of some such works that the author of the *Stalapurana* of Madura drew also his materials. Leaving aside the question of the extraordinarily long reigns attributed to many of the Pandiyans, we do not see anything impossible in the figure given. Almost all the ancient records agree in ascribing to primitive man ages far longer than those of the modern man. I do not, however, take advantage of this circumstance to lengthen the period of the supremacy of the Pandiyan dynasty, but claim only the ordinary average of 20 years per head for each of the 196 Pandiyans. This gives a total of 3920 years; supposing the last Pandiyan to have reigned in the early part of the 7th century A. D., we get the year 2620 B. C. as the commencement of the rule of the Pandiyans in the olden Madura. If so, the conclusion is inevitable, that about the year 2640 B. C. there existed Dravidian communities in India sufficiently numerous and civilized to be organized into a state, which again implies the existence of an antecedent condition of things adapted to bring about or produce these results. It would therefore seem necessary to allow a period of at least 7 or 8 centuries previous to the foundation of Madura for the development of the conditions which must be presumed to have existed at the time of the 1st Pandiyan of Madura. This brings us to about 3400 B.C, and, if our calculations be so far correct the date of Manu's flood has to be fixed somewhere about 34 centuries before the Christian Era, which seems to be neither extravagant nor impossible when viewed in the light of information we can gather on the subject from other sources, especially from the Hebrew records, as will be seen from the following table of the dates assigned to the great Novehian deluge by independent inquirers in ancient and modern times.

Jewish computation	...	2105, B. C.
Clement Alexandrinas	...	3475, B. C.
Euribius ...	...	2959, B. C.
Bede ...	...	3544, B. C.
Ursher ...	...	2349, B. C.
Hales ...	...	3153, B. C.

It will be seen from the above table that the results we have arrived at are in no way discordant with the views of more than one writer of admitted scholarship, but, on the contrary, present a strikingly historical character. It is, however, only fair to add that, according to Sir F. R. Dawson, the celebrated Canadian geologist, the figures preserved in the Hebrew records cannot be considered to have been unaffected by the imperfections of the fallible agencies by which they have been handed down to us. As regards the question of the partiality or universality of the deluge, I may here quote the words of Dr. G. Oppert and thus conclude the subject. The Professor, in his "Original Inhabitants of India," has thus remarked:—

"The fact that an ancient author, when writing the history of a country, incidently mentions that a great flood happened at the same time or previously to, or later than another event he is speaking of, is no proof that the country, whose history he is writing, was inundated by the deluge. The Biblical report is undoubtedly *a bona fide* account of an alleged universal deluge, yet, in spite of this, it is possible, yea even probable, that the so called Biblical deluge was only local, but regarded universal by the writer of the sacred book owing to his limited geographical knowledge. Even in our days, when news is quickly spread all over the world by means of telegraphic communications, it would be difficult to ascertain at once the extent of a great calamity which has befallen a distant land beyond the sphere of internal contact; how much more difficult must it have been in ancient times to obtain reliable information to the exclusiveness and ignorance of the people then living. If all the country known to a man is afflicted by an inundation, it is only natural that he should regard such a flood as universal. We know indeed of some inundations, which, in reality, only local, have been afterwards regarded universal, e. g., the great flood connected with the name of Ogyges is ascribed by some to the rising of the waters of the lake Kopais in Bœotia. Similar examples are furnished by the inundation which, caused by the river Hoangho, devastated China in the reign of the Emperor Yao, and also by the flood which, owing to the Funzha overflowing its banks, swept over the plain of Bogota in South America." (p.p. 314—315.)

A Note on the Sangam Periods.

BY THE EDITOR.

THE *Stalapurana* of Madura counts 74 Kings beginning with Kulasêkara Pandiyan and ending in Madurêswara Pandiyan, son of Kun-Pandiyan. These are the early Kings of the Pandiyan dynasty of the Modern Madura. The date of Kun-Pandiyan or Nedumaran, the last but one of the line, has been, once for all, determined to be the early part of the 7th century; and we have no records or even tradition to pronounce the existence of any Sangam during his reign. Even to the sage and poet Manikkavasagar, who belonged to the 4th century A. D., the Sangam was a thing of the past. Besides, the two celebrated works of the 2nd century A.D., viz , the *Chilappadikaram* and *Manimegalai*, contain no reference to the existence of the Sangam at the time; hence the date of the Sangam must be sought for only before the 2nd century A. D. Now, according to the tradition, the last king who patronised the third Sangam was the Pandiyan, Ugra-peru-valudi, in whose reign the famous *Tiru-Kural* is said to have been submitted to the Sangam. But, at present, we are unable to identify this King with any of the 74 Kings spoken off in the *Stalapurana*, the difficulty being of course due to the rendering into Sanskrit of the Tamil proper names by the author of the *Purana*. Nevertheless, from other sources, we are enabled to determine his date; for he is said to be the contemporary of Ilam-ched-chenni, father of Karikala whose date is fixed between 50 and 90 A. D. Thus we arrive at the conclusion that the last days of the Sangam must be sought for somewhere in the first century, and the existence of the Sangam after that date is not supported by facts. So we shall not be far from being correct in saying that the closing days of the third Sangam were but the first half of the first century of the Christian era, (*i.e.*) between 30 to 50, A.D.

We may now proceed to trace the beginnings of the Sangam. It is elsewhere stated that the Sangams have been patronised by 196 kings and have occupied a period of 3900 years, allowing 20 years per sovereign who patronised them. The first Sangam which had held its seat in the olden Madura is said to have counted 89 kings as its patrons and at last to have been destroyed by a deluge and the capital submerged into the Indian ocean. If so, these 89 kings should occupy a period of 1780 years, and if we deduct this period from the year 3900 as the beginning of the Sangam, we get the year 2120 as the date of the occurrence of the deluge. This date nearly coincides with the Jewish computation of the deluge (*i.e.*) 2105 B.C. So the year 3900 B.C. may roughly be taken as the beginning of the first Sangam, and this state of intellectual advancement is in no way improbable if we only remember that the ancient *Tamilagam* was as much a commercial and a highly civilised and cultivated country as ever. The following quotation from the *Vedic India*, by Z. A. Ragozin well answers the above statement. "In the ruins of Mugheir, the ancient Ur of Chaldea, built by Ur-Ea, the first king of united Babylonia, who ruled not less than three thousand years B.C., was found a piece of Indian *teak*. This evidence is exceptionally conclusive, because, as it happens, this particular tree is to be located with more than ordinary accuracy: it grows in Southern India (Dekkhan) where it advances close to the Malabar Coast and nowhere else; there is none to the North of the Vindya." (Vedic India, p. 305.) This shows how advanced and enterprising were the Tamilians even as early as 5000 years ago, and it will not surprise any one if we say that the Pandian dynasty was the oldest of all dynasties and that the academy founded by them in the olden Madura was the first of the Universities throughout the globe.

After the submersion of the olden Madura, Kapatapuram became the capital of the Pandyans and here it was that the second Sangam held its court. We also learn from the *Ramayana* that the capital of the Pandyans was, at the time, the same Kapatapuram. The second Sangam is said to have been supported by 59 kings who, according to our calculations, occupy a period of 1180 years. This takes us to the year 940 (2120—1180) as the date of the close of the 2nd and the commencement of the 3rd Sangam. This second capital was in its turn, so says the tradition, destroyed by an inundation; and the last king who reigned at Kapatapuram is said to have been the one who established himself in the modern Madura and there founded a Sangam or 'Kudal'. According to the *Stalapurana*, the founder of this Sangam was Ugra Pandya, better known as Papruvahana in the *Mahabharata*. He is the grandson of Malayadhvaja-Pandya whose only daughter is, according to the Mahabharata, said to have been given in marriage to Arjuna (the Sundara of the *Stalapurana*). Another fact we learn from the Mahabharata is that Arjuna met Malayadhvaja at Manalur and the old *Tiruvilaiyadal* also recognises that the Pandiyan who established his seat in the modern Madura came from Manalur which was the then capital. This suggests either that in the interval between the destruction of Kapatapuram and the foundation of the modern Madura, Manalur was occupied as a temporary capital, or, that Manalur and Kapatapuram are to be identified. Nevertheless, the site of the Pandiyan capital as described in the two great Indian Epics refer to one and the same locality. In the Ramayana, Sukriva, when describing 'Kapatam' to the Vanaras, speaks of the Pandiyan capital as standing at the junction of the Tampiraparni with the sea. And in the Mahabharata, we read that Arjuna during his pilgrimage to the South, passing through the Kalinga country, crosses the river Godavery and the Mount Mahendra of the Eastern Ghats, and then leaving behind the Kaveri, visits Manal-ur which stood near the eastern sea-shore not far from the Southern sea. While "Manal-ur" of the Mahabharata is purely a Tamil name meaning "Sandy Town", "Kapatam" of the Ramayana is, as it seems, a Sanskrit rendering of the Tamil word Alaivay. *Alaivay* (அலைவாய்) and *Turaimugam* (துறைமுகம்) are synonymous words meaning "port". The place Alaivay was a sea-port on the foot of the hill *Chendil* (செந்தில்), "house of Muruga", the war god of the Tamils, now known as Tiruchendur, a famous pilgrimage place. The city was washed away by the sea and the olden temple of Muruga is now said to lie down under the waters of the sea. We may, therefore, infer that Kapatam or Alaivay was the sea-port of the Pandiyans, well known, far and near, as an Emporium in those ancient days, and that Manalur by its side was the seat of the government and contained the house of the Pandiyans. The last Pandiyan who resided at Manalur transferred his capital to the modern Madura after the great inundation which washed away Kapatam or Alaivay, "the port", as already referred to, with a good portion of the land. This transfer of the capital from Manalur to Madura took place only just after the "Great War", *i.e.*, about 10th century B. C. The third Sangam founded at this time was presided over by 49 Pandiyans and enjoyed an unbroken prosperity for 10 centuries and at last had its close in the reign of Ugra-peruvaludi, whose date, as we have already stated, is fixed between 30 and 50 A. D. And the year 50 A. D. as that of the close of the third Sangam also marks the close of Sangam periods.

D. S.

The Antiquity of Nānjinād and Shenkōttah.

The Two Tamil Districts of Travancore.*

BY

MR. T. PONNAMBALAM PILLAI, M.R.A.S.

THE ancient history of Travancore has yet to be written, and it is a sign of the times that, with the spread of Western education, the fabulous marvels that have been described in such works as the *Kēralotpathy* and *Kerala-mahathmyam* are vanishing like the mist before the morning sun. It is to be hoped that the most orthodox of Hindus would, ere long, be in a position to discern historical facts from myths, which are mainly the products of imagination built upon slender materials. It is real patriotism to accept truth where-ever it may be found, and a careful examination of the Tamil classics will certainly throw a flood of light upon a part of the history of the chēra kingdom.

The kingdom of Travancore was carved out of the Chēra monarchy at the time of its dismemberment about the ninth century of the Christian era; in its present consolidated form it constitutes a good slice of the parent kingdom; these are facts which will not now be disputed.

Nānjinād is the southernmost end of the State of Travancore, and it is graced by the world-famous Cape Comorin which attracted the notice of such writers of antiquity as the author of the *Periplus of the Erythrean Sea*, Pliny, and Ptolemy. It, at present, consists of the taluks of

* A reprint from the Malabar Quarterly Review with kind permission.

Agastīswaram and Thōvalai, and has an area of about 210 square miles with a population of about 1,30,000 souls. It is the granary of south Travancore; and the leading ryots south of the capital own considerable areas of paddy lands. The taluk of Shenkōttah—the other Tamil appendage to the kingdom,—contains an area of about 100 square miles and a population of 40,000.

According to ancient Tamil authors, *Tamilagam*, "The Tamil-Home," which was ruled over by the three Tamil kings, Chēra, Chōla and Pāṇḍya, consisted of 13 *nàdus*, "provinces." Of these, Poolie, Kuḍam, Kuḍḍam and Vēṇ bordering on the Arabian Sea together with Karkānāḍ lying west of Kuḍam and Kuḍḍam, formed the dominion of Chēra. Mr. Kanakasabhai Pillai has proved that Travancore is composed of Kuḍḍam, a great portion of Karkānāḍ and Venaḍ, and that the last lies between Kōttayam and Cape Comorin. Nanjināḍ is the southernmost portion of it, while the sub-province of Shenkottah lies to the east of it.

The boundaries of the kingdom of Chēra were very indefinite and waxed and waned with the prowess* or otherwise of the neighbouring kings of Pāṇḍya and Chōla as is evidenced by the names of Pāṇḍyan Dam, Chōlapuram, and Muppanthal and the like. The Dam is at the head of the present irrigation system of South Travancore, and it appears to have been built by one of the Pāṇḍiyans at the time he dedicated the present shrine at Cape Comorin in honour of the virgin of virgins—the presiding deity of the place. This of course shows that that king once held sway over this part of Travancore. Chōlapuram, (close to Nagercoil) a town of great magnificence, but now in ruins, was built by one of the Chōlas,† when he was in possession of that part of the country, as can be seen from the inscription found there. Muppanthal which is situated almost at the southern frontiers

* Dutt's Ancient India, Vol. III, page 569.

† Rajendra Chola.

of the State, is supposed to have been the place where a congress of the three Tamil sovereigns and their advisers was held, after the belligerent forces had laid down their arms in order to conclude a treaty of peace. Chēra also appears to have led his victorious army into his neighbours' territories and held a firm grip over certain portions of them. There are evidences to point to the rule of Chēra or Travancore over the taluks of Nāngunēry, Ambāsamudram, Tencausy and Sangarnayinār-Koil in the Tinnevelly District. The inscriptions in the Tiru-kurum-gudy temple in the Nangunery taluk demonstrate the fact. The name of Chēren Mā-dēvi, the chief town of Ambāsamudram, is a significant proof of the connection between Chēra and that place. The temple of Malayankulam with its adjacent property in the same taluk is still owned by Travancore, and the fact is proof positive of the sway of Chēra or his successors over the regions about it. This portion of the Tinnevelly District was exchanged for a small bit of territory between Shenkottah and Puliyarai, and in calculating the revenue of both the places, as the latter yielded Rs. 30 and odd more than the other, that amount is being paid into the British treasury at Tencausy by the Travancore Government. The taluks of Tencausy and Sangaranayinār-Koil are so intertwined with Shenkottah that all the three taluks must have once owed allegiance to one and the same ruler. The large establishments maintained in Courtalam and the Sangaranayinār-Koil temples, and the vast amount of money spent there daily by Travancore, may also partly prove the connection between the western part of the Tinnevelly District, which was the *Tenpandi-nad* according to Tamil writers, and Travancore.

Amongst the three Tamil kings, the Pāṇḍyans were the chief patrons of learning, and the three Tamil *Sangams* or Academies were maintained by them one after another between long intervals. It has also been demonstrated that the closing session of the last or the third Academy was held during the first century of the Christian era. There are numerous valuable works written by the members of this literary society and handed down to us. Amongst these are two anthologies containing poems by various poets of eminence, selected and edited by famous poets of later generations. These works are called *Agananuru* (inner or esoteric four hundred) and *Purananuru* (outer or exoteric four hundred), each containing four hundred *stanzas*. These verses are generally in praise of the three kings of the Tamil country and other men who have played a prominent part on the stage of Tamil history. Amongst the latter were tributary princes, prime ministers, generals, courtiers and others.

It appears from *Purananuru* that Nānjināḍ was once ruled by a prince styled Nānjil Porunan.* The word *Porunan* signifies a king; but in the present instance it appears to have been the family name of the hero whom the original commentator of the anthology calls Nanjil Vaḷḷuvan. The term *Valluvan* is generally applied to the priestly class amongst the Pariahs, but in Nānjināḍ its former ruler is known at present as Nānjil Kuravan. The Kuravas are a nomadic race, and seem to be connected with the aboriginal Kurumbas. They are generally supposed to be experts in surgical operations connected with the human ear. According to the traditionary account that is current at the place, it seems that the province was made a grant of in favour of the founder of the dynasty in return for a skilful operation of the kind referred to above on the ear of an infant princess of the Pāṇḍyan family. The Periya or Valiyavettil Mudaliar at Alagiapāndiapuram plays a prominent part on all ceremonial occasions, and enjoys certain privileges over his fellow-citizens granted to him by the crown. He is supposed to be the descendant of the last prime minister of the Prince of Nānjil. Even at subsequent times, this family appears to have been honoured with the grant of golden ploughs and other marks of royal appreciation. A hillock

* Stanzas 137, 140 and 380, *Purananuru.*

between Alágiapāndiapuram and Kadukarai, in the Thovalai taluk, is pointed out as the place where the Porunan held his court. The discovery of gold coins and other momentoes of his rule seems to confirm the popular notion regarding his capital.

It is not known how Nānjinād came to bear its present name—whether the ruler lent his name to it or the province gave its name to him. The Tamil word *Nanjil* means a plough as is evident from stanza 19 of *Purannnuru*. It may be that this part of the country derived its name from the large extent of rice-fields there. For, in stanzas 137 and 139 of the Anthology Orusirai-Peyarinār and Maruthan-iḷa-nāganār speak of the uncommon fertility of the soil, the consequent superfluity of tilling it, and the large volume of water that is discharged into the sea carrying in its train flowers of variegated colours. The poet also refers to a small waterfall which is evidently Olakaruvy, not far away from Alagiapāndiapuram, and the large number of granite hills. In stanza 138 the poet speaks of the large number of beasts that roam in the forests, and the different kinds of fishes that are to be found in the water courses. On the authority of *Chilapathikâram*, we find that the system of catching elephants by means of the pit-system was in vogue in the Chēra country at the time of which we are writing, and the Nānjil-Porunan, having entrapped a *plethora* of them, did not know how to dispose of them. For, we see from stanza 140 that when a poor minstrel went to him for relief with his starving family, he presented him with a huge beast which appeared as "a towering hill in the midst of a dense jungle." The poet, of course, mildly rebukes the low-born prince for his selfish inconsiderateness in looking only to his own reputation regardless of the circumstances under which the donee sought his help. Even to-day the northern portion of Nānjinād forms a safe and convenient asylum for herds of these animals. In the same stanza and in the 380th, the poets refer to the Nānjil hill stocked with jack trees that yield the most delicious of fruits. Though the whole of Nāñjināḍ is not fit for the healthy growth of fruit trees of this species, the Nanjil hill and the places north-east of it, are admirably adapted for their cultivation, and they flourish in groves in these localities. From the foregoing description we feel no doubt that *Purananuru* refers to the modern Nāñjināḍ, the southernmost province of Travancore; but we are inclined to believe that its area was larger than what it is at present, stretching from the Pothiya hill to the sea in a south-westerly direction.

In the preceding paragraphs we have referred to the line of princes who exercised kingly power over Nāñjināḍ as *Nanjil Porunan* and added that, at the present day, the people of the place refer to them as *Nanjil Kuravan.* We may further state that, notwithstanding the low origin of that royal house, the people speak of the defunct family with veneration. We called this petty ruler a tributary prince on the authority of stanza 139 of *Purananuru.* For, the poet addressing the Porunan says, "Your king will give you all that you want, and you are certain to lay down your very life for his sake." But we are not in a position to say positively to whom he owed allegiance. Pandit Swaminatha Aiyar, the talented and most erudite editor of *Purananuru*, says that the Porunan was a feudal vassal, rendering military service to the Chēra, and I believe he has his authority to say so. On the other hand, Mr. Kanakasabhai Pillai, another great authority, says that he owed allegiance to the Pāṇḍyan. It is our impression that this country of the Porunan now acknowledged Chēra and now Pandya as its supreme lord according to the prowess of each, though its existence as a separate principality was due to the magnanimous liberality of the latter.

In the earlier portion of this paper reference has already been made to certain places in the Tinnevelly District as having once been an integral part of Travancore or the Chera kingdom. There is so much in common between Nāngunēri and Nānjināḍ that it is probable that both the provinces owed allegiance to one and the same ruler. The people of one place have relations in the other even at the present day, and it is generally said that some of the best families in south Travancore went from the other place. When the inhabitants of Nānjināḍ adopted the *Marumakkathayam* system as their law of inheritance in order to demonstrate their loyalty to the then sovereign of Travancore, some of them had violently to tear away from their blood relations in the Nānguneri taluk, and though no inter-marrying and inter-dining are kept up at present, still the relations at one place visit those in the other in remembrance of their past ties. There is a class of people called the "Paravur Sorupani" at Paravur, eight miles south of Quilon, who are so very exclusive that their women seldom mix with out-siders. They claim to have emigrated from Kalacaud in the Nānguneri taluk, and in evidence thereof they use certain Tamil expressions which are peculiarly their own. The other portions of the Tinnevelly District to which reference was made elsewhere, however, must have belonged to some other province of Travancore, and not to Nānjināḍ.

The same work *Purananuru*, which speaks of the Nanjil principality, also speaks of a chief by name Ay (ஆய்).* His capital was Ayecudy,† and the hill which gave him prominence over his compeers was the sacred Pothiya, the supposed residence of the Rishi Agathya, the author of the first grammar and other works in Tamil. The verses above referred to not only give a glowing description of the country ruled over by the line of Ay Princes (which also as in the case of Porunan, was a family name), but also speaks of their acts of philanthropy and of the valiant deeds of one of its princes—Andiran by name, in driving the Kongas into the western sea. Now, naturally, the question turns upon

* See *Purananuru* verses 127—136.

† Verses 132, 241, 374 and 375, *Ibid.*

the identity of the country ruled over by them. There is a small town known by the name of Ayecudy, seven miles from Shenkottah, and four miles from Tencausy. From its position and the ruins that are to be found here and there, we are of opinion that this is the place referred to in the *Purananuru* as the capital of the principality of Ay. It is not more than thirty miles from the Pothiya hill which has been referred to in the poems as belonging to this king. The area on the west must have extended as much as it had extended on the east up to the Pothiya hill. This means that the limits of this tributary state reached Punalore and Pathanapuram and perhaps even up to Pandalam, where the descendants of Ay live to-day. Mr.Kanakasabhai Pillai says,* "South of Vaikkara or Kottayam, Ptolemy places the country of Aioi. This was the territory of the Ay, a family of chiefs of the Pothiya hills who were great patrons of poets. The towns Elankon, Kottiara and Bammala may be identified with the modern Vilavancode, Kottar and Ponmana." This description places the principality of Ay in Vēnād, and as already mentioned, it must have extended on the east up to the Pothiya hill, and on the west as far as Panthalam or even further beyond the territories ruled over by the later Rajahs of Kāyancolam and Kottārakarai. I should, therefore, think that Elankone meant Elukone, eleven miles from Quilon, Kottiara, Kottarakarai, and Bammala, Punalore or Pathanapuram. Mr.Kanakasabhai Pillai has told us† that Ptolemy never visited India, and that his accounts were drawn up from the reports of traders, who visited India from Alexandria and other parts of the Roman Empire. As the chief article of their trade was pepper, they could have directed their footsteps only to places where that commodity could have been obtained in plenty. Vilavancode and Kottar are not pepper producing districts, and the quantity of pepper obtained from Ponmanai and its environs is indeed small. But there is not the least doubt that it is

* The Tamils: 1800 Years Ago, page 50.

† The Tamils: 1800 Years Ago, page 20.

obtained largely at Elukone, Kottarakarai, and the places about them. We have already made mention of the extent of the principality of Ay on the eastern side of Travancore up to the Pothiya hill. The fact of Chēranmādēvi, the principal town of Ambasamudram Taluq, in Tinnevelly, bearing the name of the chief Queen of Chēra, and Malayāmkulam belonging to Travancore at present goes to show that other places about them were once included in the country ruled over by Ay (ஆய்) and therefore by the suzerain Chēra, whose heir is the present Ruler of Travancore.

The people belonging to Shenkottah and its neighbourhood, regard the Panthalam royal family with some reverence. It is generally a custom with Hindus that, when a person proposes to perform an important ceremony such as a marriage in his house, he intimates the fact in due form to the King by the presentation of betel leaves, areca nut, sugar, lime fruits, spices and flowers, and invokes his blessing. Some of the people of Shenkottah and about it still continue to pay this empty homage to the chief of that family. This, of course, means that their ancestors must have held sway over those parts. It is supposed that they were the kinsmen of the Paṇḍyan royal family. They might either have been relations, or dependants, and the principality of Ay must have been granted for services rendered to the Paṇḍyan royal house. We have elsewhere stated that the Panthalam family emigrated to Travancore through the Ghauts.* Even after the downfall of the Paṇḍyan house, some of the members of this family remained at Madura attached to the Naick kings, but stress of circumstances compelled them to take refuge in Travancore, and according to traditionary accounts, the members of that house are said to have moved from Ayakudy to Elathure, from there to Kōniyur, through the Achankōvil pass, and finally from there to Panthalam. At a later date Samboor Vadakarai was in

* The Malabar Quarterly Review, Vol. III.

the possession of the Raja of Kāyancolam and the town of Shenkottah in that of the Rajah of Kottarakarai, but we shall not dwell on that subject in the present paper. Here it is enough to state that there is a place called Ayakudy belonging to a Naick Zemindar in the Madura District, but it is not contiguous to the Pothiya hills and does not answer to the description of Ptolemy and *Purananuru*.

It requires no proof to convince our readers that Tamil is spoken at Nānjinād and Shenkottah at present and that they are, therefore, the Tamil speaking provinces of the Malayalam State of Travancore. We have already stated that the close of the last session of the third Academy was during the first century of the Christian era, and the poets whose verses find place in the collection of *Purananuru* were all members of that literary assembly. But it is too much to say that all of them—about one hundred and sixty in number—lived at one and the same time. Some of them must have flourished earlier, and some during the first century. This is also the view taken by Mr. Kanakasabhai Pillai. If the poets who immortalised the royal house of Nanjil Porunan and Ay belonged to the first century and times anterior to it, the origin of the two principalities must have been earlier still.

Thus, the king of ancient Travancore, an offspring of more hoary Chēra, who consolidated his dominions and made his mark before "1800 Years Ago," along with his other two brother Tamil sovereigns, secured Nānjinād and Shenkottah which included in them a greater area of territory than at present, most likely from sea to sea, and probably also Kakkur close to Ramnad where Travancore owns property at present.

Sage Pavanandhi, Critic and Teacher.

BY

Mr. M. S. PURANALINGAM PILLAI, B. A., L. T.

THE devotion of the Jains to the enrichment and extention of Tamil Literature cannot be overrated. Among their immortal works may be mentioned the *Nannul*, composed by the Jain ascetic, Pavaṇandhi' of Janakapuram, about Conjeveram, at the request of Sīya Gangan, a tributary prince under Kulôthunga Chola III. Though based on Tholkāppiam, the oldest Tamil grammar extant, and though the prefatory lines refer to the work having been perfected in all its five parts of letters, words, matter, prosody and rhetoric, the renowned and most popular work of the ascetic treats of the first two sections alone; and whatever be the fate of the other three parts devoured by time or by white ants, the fragment shows what a clear thinker, analyst and systematiser the author was and how the lapse of seven centuries has not robbed it of a tithe of its original freshness and charm. The exordium to this excellent treatise affords materials to us wherewith to form a true estimate of the sage in his double capacity of critic and teacher.

As a critic he has laid down canons of criticism which, examined under the search-light of modern works on the subject, are a medley of processes of thought and diction, but, looked at with the spectacles of seven hundred years ago, speak volumes of the author's keen judgment and judicious selection of materials. According to him a classic is god-given or god-inspired, supplemental or derivative; and a supplemental classic is marked off from the derivative by the degree and extent of their divergence from the original in respect of subject matter and treatment. If the divergence be small and in minor matters, it is called supplemental; if large and in important items, it is known as derivative classic. But both supplemental and derivative classics are bound to quote the textual *sutras* without garbling or mutilation. Every classic is intended to teach virtue, wealth, pleasure and bliss, and to embody one of the seven objects contemplated by the author. It is the critic's first function to see if the composer of a classical work has fallen in or out with the long-established truths or doctrines, or accepted and rejected them in part, or refuted them, or has established a brand new truth, or has, in cases of dilemma when doctors disagreed, embraced a cause most convincing to him or has picked holes in the writings of others, or has expounded his own view of a matter independent of the light shed upon it by others. After he has made out the *motif* or the rational of a classic, the critic then begins to sit in judgment upon it with a view to display its beauties and to ferret out its flaws, and demonstrates that his function is not, as it is popularly imagined, one-sided, *viz.* the detection of weak points; but two sided, discovering faults and excellences alike. The fault that an expert eye lights upon in examining a new work as it does upon specks in precious gems are ten in number. Excessive brevity leads to obscurity. Diffuseness is its antepodes. Frequent repetitions induce disgust and tediousness. Inconsistency is flat contradiction. Impurity consists in the use of foreign, slang, vulgar or provincial terms in a dignified composition. Ambiguity leaves the mind in doubt as to meaning. Verbosity is applied to a collection of words full of sound and fury and signifying nothing. Digression is a disproportionate expansion of a subordinate idea which distracts the mind from the main topic. By languid close is meant the gradual weakening of the strength in thought and expression as the work comes to a close. Pleonasm is a redundant use of words which needs to be lopped off. A good classic must then shun these faults: over-brevity, diffuseness, iteration, inconsistency, impurity, ambiguity, verbosity, digression, flagging, pleonasm; and it must possess the ten beauties enumerated below: brevity, perspicuity, interest, exquisite expression, depth, good mapping of the subject, systematic ordering of the topics, pregnant significance, conformity with good usage, choice illustrations.

The critic's next function is to examine the use or emyloyment of the *yuktis* or devices, which are thirty-two as mentioned in the *Nannul*. These include the afore-mentioned seven topics, ten faults and ten beauties' to which are added five points anew. The theme must be stated at the outset. The old and archaic things must be brushed off and new ones espoused. Testimony and authority must be relied on. Reference must be made, prospective and reprospective. Relevency and cogency must be demonstrated. All these thirty-two devices were pressed into service in the composition of a memorable work, and the *sutras* of which it consisted required commentaries or *bhashyas* on account of their laconism. Since the *bhashyas* often formed part and parcel of old classics and were classics in themselves, the critic was enjoined the additional duty of pronouncing his opinion and passing his judgment on the worth of the commentaries, in respect of each of their fourteen characteristics, *viz.*, pure text, purport, construing, word meaning, paraphrasing, citing parallel passages, questioning, answering queries, adding fresh explanatory matter, free exposition, the relevancy of the Sutras comprising chapters or sections, giving the meaning boldly in doubtful cases, the result of this, and quoting authority. If the commentaries comprise a few of these points, as purport, lexicon, illustration and catechism, they are called *kandikais* or brief *bhashyas*; if they exemplify all and are lucid in their exposition they are known as elaborate or diffuse *bhashyas* or *Vrithis*.

The Pedagogics of Pavaṇandhi fall into two main divisions, (*a*) the qualifications of the teacher and the qualities of the pupil, and (*b*) how to teach and to learn. A teacher, according to the sage, must be a man of high birth. Those that have risen from the ranks have generally none of the ring of magnanimity and broad-mindedness; and, however high their intellectual culture, the narrowness of their heart peeps out at times and tinges all their sayings and doings. He must have a rich endowment of good will and mercy and patience. Where these virtues are wanting, the schoolmasters are the veritable bretheru of Mr. Squees in Dicken's Nicholas Nickleby, and their schools are none other than Do-the-boys-halls. Where love rules, the rod has no place. The impatience of modern teacher is much to be regretted, and the deterioration in the quality of the present day product is due to the lack of this essential element of success. Good temper counts more than intellectual equipment, and a knowledge of the ways of the world is a necessary supplement and corrective to the bookish or ideal view of life and its doings. It is a common reproach that the Schoolmaster is an unpractical man. The prince of dramatists and the prince of novelists have not spared him. A teacher must be in touch with everything that goes on in the world and is expected to be a walking cyclopedia. A clouded mind is worse than a vacant brain. Above all a teacher must have faith in God, respect himself, and command the respect of the world. Lack of self-respect leads to loss of public esteem and the status of the teacher has gone down for lack of busbyism.* Pavanandhi has

* Dr. "Richard Bushy" (1606—1695), the most famous of English Schoolmasters, was appointed Head-master of Westminster School in 1640, and discharged the duties of his office until his death. He is the type of pedagogues alike for learning, assiduity and the application of the birch. As a most successful teacher for over half a century, he bred up the greatest

compared a teacher to the earth, a mountain, a balance, and a flower. Like the earth, his knowledge must be wide and deep and solid, his patience exemplary, and his teaching productive. Like the mountain his intellectual wealth must be inexhaustible and varied, his eminence conspicuous and unassailable, and his generosity disinterested and unrequitable. Like the balance,he must resolve doubts, be true, just and impartial to all. Like the flower, he must draw the world to himself by his personal fascination, amiable manners, and *sine qua non* character. The Sage deprecates incommunicativeness, meanness, deceit, envy, avarice, intimidation on the part of a teacher and likens such an incompetent teacher to a pot of marbles, a rough palmyra, a cotton-stuffed Demi-John, and a slanting coconut tree. The *immethodical* teacher is like a jar of marbles and works without a plan. The *inaccessible* teacher is like the rough-barked palmyra whose fruit cannot be reached unless it drops of itself. The *imperfect* teacher is like the Demi-John, hard to put in and hard to take out. The *negligent* teacher, like the slanting cocoanut palm, helps strangers and not his own benefactors. A good teacher selects a suitable place, chooses a fit hour, invokes god on a *dais* and imparts his knowledge in a clear and methodical manner, amiably, willingly and directly with a due regard to the capacity of the learner. The learner may be his own son, the son of his *guru*, a prince, one who will pay well, or who will be serviceable to him in the years to come, or who is very intelligent. Learners are of three orders. The Wranglers or the topmen are discriminative like the swan and reflective like the cow. The optimes or middling class are resceptive like the sand and unoriginal in their talk like the parrot. The wooden spoons or the lowest resemble cracked pots that

number of learned scholars that ever adorned any age or nation. Once when the Sovereign of the land paid a visit to his school, Dr. Busbhy took his Majesty over the class-rooms with his hat on, and when he was asked how he had dared to neglect that politeness which was due to kings, he replied that he was the monarch of his realm and that within the four corners of his little kingdom, his pupils should not know that there was a greater man than he.

let out-everything, are capricious like goats, muddling like buffaloes, and retentive of dregs like the ghee-strainers. The Sage proceeds to tell us who are unfit to learn and to whom no instruction should be imparted. They are the lazy, the sleepy, the indigent, the tipsy, the conceited, the dull-headed, the lusty, the sickly, the thievish, the sulky, the despondent, the cruel, the vile and the lying. The reclamation of these unworthies is engaging the attention of the modern educators and statesmen; and as there is a soul of goodness in things evil, the good points in them must be taken advantage of and improved lest they be damned as irretrievables and incurables. According to the sage, punctual attendance, willing, cheerful and implicit obedience, thirst for knowledge, mental concentration, a ready ear, an eager mind and a retentive memory are the distinguishing marks of good pupils, which he calls their duties.

The next section of his Pedagogics deals with the methods of study. Every careful student aims at a mastery of the usages of the languages he learns, revises and re-revises what he has learnt, digests aud assimilates what he has received, repairs to his master to clear his doubts and to bring on what is subliminal, seeks the society of enlightened men, and discusses with them what he takes to be difficult or knotty or intricate. A study of the usages is of greater importance than the parrot-like learning of words and their meanings. Constant revision has a fixative value and facilitates clear understanding. By going to the master often, the pupil gains opportunities to know at first hand what is to be learnt in cases of doubt and difficulty and to revive in his mind what has passed into the limbo of things forgotten. Digestion and assimilation are operations as essential to the health of the mind as they are to bodily health. Undigested or ill-digested crudities breed diseases. To be in constant touch with learned men is a way of adding to and improving one's stock, and to debate and discuss with them clarifies one's powers of understanding and makes things otherwise formidable, very easy to learn and to keep. No pupil can attain perfection by merely sitting at the feet of his *guru* and gleaning his sapience. He must supplement what he has gathered from his teacher by moving in learned societies and when he turns out a teacher his progress approaches completion, and when he makes a *debut* on a public platform he becomes perfect in thought, word and action. Such a perfect scholar has the greatest respect for his master follows him like his shadow, does whatever pleases him, and lives a virtuous life.

Thus, I have run over Pavanandhi's art of criticism and his pedagogy pointing out *en route* that his critical canons are a jumble of the fundamental processes of composition, and that his pedagogy, bearing as it does all the marks of imperfection of the age in which he lived, offer some good points and happy suggestions to the modern thoughtful Educationist who is bent on revolutionising the current system of godless or irreverent Education and who hopes to plant in its place a system of body-and-soul-saving learning with the hearty co-operation of apt, disinterested, and self-sacrificing teachers, and docile, attentive and reverent pupils.

DRAVIDIAN COINS

BY

DEWAN BAHADUR T. M. RENGACHARIAR, B.A.

AND

DEWAN BAHADUR T. DESIKACHARIAR, B.A., B.L. M.R.A.S.

I.

TO trace the growth and development of the Monetary System in South India, we have to go back to the days of the Pandyas and the Cholas. Their coinage was mainly in copper and silver. Flat thin rectangular pieces in silver have been found both in Tinnevelly and Madura, bearing the impression of Buddhistic devices "punched" on them with a seal or seals. The appearance on their reverse of a symbol which forms the characteristic feature of the rectangular copper coins of Madura and Tinnevelly, point to the obvious inference that the coinage in both the metals is attributable to the same power, though the punch-marked silver coins must be assigned to an earlier age than that of the die-struck copper coins.

Similiar coins in silver have been found in all parts of India. "They have been discovered among the ashes of the men who constructed the primitive tombs known as *kulis* (or kistaevens) of the south and unearthed from the ruins of buried cities in excavating the head waters of the Ganges Canal. In all parts, from the Sandarbans of the Ganges to the frontiers of Afghanistan they turn up from time to time." And more recently they have been reported to occur among the finds of the excavations in the ruined city of Anuradhapura in Ceylon.

From their occurrence over such a wide area and in such great numbers one might suppose that there was some uniform standard or unit of currency adopted everywhere in India. In the imperfect state of our knowledge of the ancient Indian Monetary System, no definite statement can be made about what exactly led to this apparent uniformity in the size and the devices of these coins. We can do no more than indicate the nature of the speculation on the subject leaving further research to throw more light on so obscure a topic.

The suggestion has often been advanced that the silver coins were the *purana* (ancient-elding) which formed the silver representative of the primitive seminal exponent of value named the *kalanju* approxinately equal to 45 or 50 grains. There is no doubt of the existence of a certain relation between the weights and measures and the money of a country and the suggestion "that the monetary system of S. India is of indigenous origin based on rude, seminal and testaceous exponents of value which have been exchanged for definite metallic counters" has much to recommend it; but having regard to the varying weights of these silver pieces, it cannot be asserted as beyond doubt, that they represented the silver *kalanju*.

Another theory proceeds on the hypothesis that the Dravidians borrowed the Phœnician unit of the Drachma weighing 57 grains, which tallies with the weight of the punch-marked specimens obtained in Northern India. For many centuries before the Christian era, it is certain that Dravidian merchants had developed such a degree of maritime- and commercial enterprise as to tempt them to undertake voyages across the seas to distant countries, and it is believed by some scholars that it was they, who becoming acquainted with an alphabetic writing derived from the Presemetic-Accadians north of the Euphrates valley, brought the script to India, being thus the first to introduce the art of writing into India. Such an adventurous people were not slow to introduce into their country, a metrical standard with which they became acquainted in their foreign transactions. "As the Phœnicians had penetrated everywhere establishing with their accustomed enterprise their factories on almost every coast, they soon discovered the metallic wealth of the land and began to work for the first time the veins of silver which had lain for ages unsuspected in the mountains." The silver plates from Tarshish were imported into India by the Phœnicians to buy Indian gold and in such transactions they must have adopted their own unit of the Drachma. It was not strange then that copying the example, the Tamils cut the silver sheets into small pieces, weighing approximately as much as the Phœnician unit and had the same passed as measures of value easily resolvable into a given quantity of gold. In course of time the silver pieces would come to the stamped with some authoritative mark or marks and with the change of the ruling power or the reception of a prince into the domains of another sovereign or through other causes, various seals would be imprinted on the same piece, in some instances one seal being superimposed over the other. This origin of the punch-marked silver coins at once explains the uniformity in size and the occurrence over such a wide area as from the Himalayas to Cape Comorin and the Island of Ceylon of the silver coins in question. They are supposed to have been the *Karshas* current at the time of Buddha, and the period of their currency synchronises with the palmy days of the Phœnician trade, six or seven centuries before the Christian era.

In a communication to the Royal Asiatic Society by Captain T. B. Jervis of the Engineer Corps in 1835, that talented Engineer essays to establish a relation between the *Massa* or *Masha* which is the basis of the *tola* and *seer* with the weight of a pound as deduced from a primitive universal standard, *viz.*, a pendulum vibrating seconds, one half of which roughly is the primitive cubit. "This pendulum cubed, and multiplied" into the weight of a cubic inch of distilled water, each cubic inch weighing 252·984 grains Troy, divided into 48 or 28 parts, furnishes an explanation of all the weights of whatever kind whether money or gross weight throughout the world in all ages." By a manipulation of the figures which it is needless here to reproduce, it is demonstrated that ancient *hun* or *pon* and a tenth of it the *fanam* were both multiples or sub-multiples of the *Massa* of 15 and odd grains each *hun* being also half of the Drachma of 109 grains.

Neither the weights of the punch-marked silver coins, nor those of the silver pieces of the period of the Chola ascendancy, furnish any clue as to the correctness of any of these theories. The coins of Raja Raja weigh 90 grains; those of Uttama Chola 85 grains and those of Kulothunga 70 grains.

We possess in the South India Inscriptions a fairly accurate record of the weights and measures current in the period after the 9th century A. D. during which the Cholas suddenly rose into prominence and were for a time supreme in Southern India.

An inscription in Mammalapuram (the Seven Pagodas) of the illustrious Ko Raja-raja Raja Kesari Varman, relating to a contract for the new division of their lands by the citizens of the town provides as follows:—

"Among those who are without land and are over the age of sixteen—from those who are engaged in trade half a *Kalanju* of gold (*pon*), from those who work for hire one eighth of a *pon* and for (each) turn as ploughmen (?) three-eighths of a (*pon*) shall be taken at the end of the year. From those who do not submit to this contract further twenty-five *Kalanjus* of gold shall be taken besides a fine. In an inscription of the Virupaksheswara Temple at Vembatu near Velur in the North Arcot District the value of property is calculated throughout in *Kula* pramanas or *Kulas* of gold (*pon*) and in *panas* and it is recorded that 242 *Kula* pramanas of gold and 41⅛ *panas* are equal to 36 *Kovais* of gold and 5⅛ *panas*.

In the Kanchipuram inscriptions of Madurai-Konda-Ko-parakesarivarman, we find the penalty for a person not carrying out a charitable obligation was the payment of "one *manjadi* of gold daily to the king who is then ruling" or "one eighth of a *pon* daily paid in Court" or "one *Kunri* of gold daily paid in Court." In another inscription of the 3rd year of Ko Raja Kesarivarman, from the same place, it is recorded that the villagers of Manalūr pledged themselves to furnish oil for a lamp from the interest of a sum of money received from the royal Treasury said to be "eighteen *Kalanju*, ten *Manjadis* and one *Kunri* of gold."

In the Raja Raja inscriptions of Tanjore the weight of the jewels presented to the Temple is expressed in *Kalanju*, *Manjadi* and *Kunri* according to standard weights made of stone and preserved in the shrine of the god Adavattan, also called Dakshina Meru Vitankar. Silver seems to have been also weighed in *Kalunjus* and *Manjadi* and rated just in the same way as gold and the precious stones and pearls. Copper seems to have been weighed in *palas*, a copper water pot (*kudam*) being recorded as weighing three thousand eighty three *palas*.

From other inscriptions we find that the gold *kasu* was half a *madurantaka madai*, that an *akkam* 1/12 of a *kasu*.

The purchasing power of a *kasu* is found to be 2 *kalams* of paddy or 3 sheep or 1200 plantains or 7/20 *Kalanju* of gold.

Besides the *madai*, the *kasu*, the *kovai* and the *akkam* reference is found to another term, signifying token or a weight, if not a coin, as in the instance of a payment of so many *Kanam* a day into court as a fine.

Moreover two kinds of *pons* are also referred to as "Urk-kachchemmai—pon" and tulainirai—pon which are equivalents of so many kalanjus gold.

Whether there was any definite ratio between the value of gold and silver or whether the value of gold fluctuated with that of any other commodity and was determined in silver are matters upon which it would be rash to hazard even a conjecture.

The only Pandyan gold coin known to us is a tiny piece ascribable to "Sundara Paṇḍya," but it is imposible to locate the age of the monarch who issued the coin. The period of Chola ascendancy has examples of the coins of Raja Raja Chola in gold, and gold coins or more than one denomination in the Chola-Chalukyan period.

Side by side with coins or tokens in the precious metals the Pāṇḍyans possessed a currency in copper, which comprised die-struck coins unlike the punch-marked silver adverted to already. They resolve themselves into two varieties, rectangular coins which bear Buddhistic devices and a later variety of coins which are round and bear Vishnavite or Sivite emblems.

The former of the Buddhist coins occur at least in five denominations, the smallest weighing 30 grains while the heaviest coins weigh 144 grains, the intermediate weights are 40, 60 and 80 grains.

Writing about the economic conditions in Buddhist India, Professor Rhys Davids makes the following observations which are instructive in the investigation of this copper coinage. "The older system of traffic by batten had entirely passed away never to return. The latter system of a currency of standard and token coins issued and regulated by Government authority had not yet arisen. Transactions were carried on, values estimated, and bargains struck in terms of the *Kahapana*, a square coppor coin weighing about 146 grains and guaranteed as to weight and fineness by punch-marks, by private individuals. Whether these punch-marks are tokens of merchants or of guilds or simply of the bullion dealer is not certain." These observations are of interest, relating as they do to the coins occuring in Northern India and based on the examination of the Buddhist records unconnected with the Tamils who, by the geographical position of their country, had for over twenty centuries maintained their political independence in the southern most portion of the Peninsula. It is remarkable that as in the silver punch-marked coins the size, weight, and devices resemble very much those of the coins occuring in portions of India remote from the Tamil Kingdoms and having nothing in common expect perhaps the religion of Buddha.

With the change in the shape of the old variety and the introduction of the symbols of a different faith, the practice of issuing "Kahapanas" of 144 grains was discontinued. The Monetary System seems to have been remodelled, and henceforth no silver coins were probably issued and coins in copper of various denominations judging by the weights of specimens now available were put in circulation. The average weights of the various sizes are 58, 30, 14 and 7½ grains.

The change from the square coinage of the Buddhist period to the latter round coinage with Vishnavite and Sivite emblems and the adoption of an apparently different standard of weight must have been brought about by causes that cannot solely be looked for, in the revival of the Puranic faith in India. In the early centuries of the Christian era there was a large influx of foreign merchants and a considerable quantity of Roman aurei and dinarii must have been imported by them into India for purposes of merchandise and indeed we read of gifts in dinarii for the maintenance of lamps in temples. Small copper coins were also locally minted by a colony or colonies of foreigners and it is not improbable that the change in the shape and weight of the coins of the Tamil Kings had some sort of connection with their intercourse with Rome.

Of the copper coins of the period of the Chola ascendancy the most numerous are the copper *kasus* of Raja Raja which occur in three varieties, the largest of them weighing 90 grains. The coins of the Chola-Chalukyan period present yet a further change in the weights of the largest specimens which on an average weigh 74 grs.

It will be evident from an examination of the weights of the various copper coins found in S. India that the task of arriving at a uniform standard for them is by no means a safe or easy one. Various factors are calculated to introduce confusion in any speculation bearing on the matter not the least of which are the discrepancies in the weights of the coins of the several denominations viewed from the stand-point of any of the various theories put forward to explain and fix the primitive unit of currency. The mention of a *kasu*, a *panam* or a *pon* in Tamil literature and inscriptions is of little import as connoting the idea of any definite value as the use of words of similar significance, *viz.* ,the *purana swarana* and *hyranya* in ancient Sanskrit and Pali literature, with reference to the coins and tokens in the precious metals.

II. PANDIAN COINS.

The Coin collector in South India cannot fail to be struck by the large variety of issues in copper that abound in such great numbers in and about the sites of the ancient Pandyan capitals of Korkai (Tinnevelly District) and Madura. Equally remarkable is the curious feature of the Pandyan coinage that silver coins were either never issued, or were issued so sparingly that they have not come down to us at all. It is however, not free from doubt whether the silver, irregularly shaped, punchmarked pieces often found along with Pandyan coins were currrent in the Pandyan Kingdom during the prevalence of Bhuddism in India. A not dissimilar paucity is observable in the silver currency of the Vijayanagar Kingdom, the prolificness of whose gold issues, is testified to by the innumerable *pagodas* and half *pagodas* available in the market even at the present day, while not more than three or four silver 'Vijanagar,' possibly forgeries, are known to S. I. Numismatists.

Pandyan gold coins are met with but rarely and are generally ill-designed fanams bearing on the obverse the figure of a man and on the reverse the legend, which if complete, may be read as "Sundara Pandyan." The late Lieut General Pearse in his papers bequeathed to the Government Central Museum gave the following description of a gold coin which he procured in the London Market for sixteen shillings :—

Obverse :—Two fishes looking downwards on a fish lying horizontally: above is an alligator. Two standards or dwaja stambas or pillars of Victory are supporters to the central design.

Reverse :—Three lines of old bold *nagari* characters which have not been read. Col. Mackenzie noticing a coin of the same description attributes it to the ancient Pandyas.

Similar coins were found in South Canara which were probably issued by a branch of the Pandyas who had settled there.

Judging from the small number of gold issues that have hitherto found their way into Coin Cabinets, it appears to be a fair inference to draw that the Pandyan kings issued comparatively fewer gold coins than other dynasties of the South. It cannot however be forgotten that the Pandyans virtually ceased to be a ruling power nearly 500 years ago, that in India there is always a tendency to send gold in every form into the melting pot for satisfying the demand for jewellery in the precious metal and that it was by no means improbable that during the Mohammadan interregnum in Malabar, (the old name for S. India) and the long Nayakka rule the gold coins of the Pandyan Kings found their way into the gold-smith's crucible and graced in time as jewels the persons of the fair devotees of Meenakshi.

By far the most interesting issues of the Pandyan dynasty, are those in copper, which seem to have been struck in such abundant profusion that they are met with now, after the lapse of centuries, in the Madura country and are picked out of the bed of the Vaigai or the fields near Korkai after a shower of rain.

The fish was the emblem of the Pandyans just as the tiger was that of the Cholas, the bow of the Cheras and the boar of the Chalukyas. Those which appear to be the earliest issues do not bear the emblem of the fish, but are square pieces, bearing well executed figures of the elephant and, the bull, on their obverse associated with many devices peculiar to the Bhuddhist faith like the wheel, the sacred tree, the khumba and the chaitya while on their reverse there invariably appears a diagram, by some supposed to represent the plan of Madura Town with the river Vaigai. The mounted figures on the elephant on some of the coins and the artistic finish and the perfect form of the images in all of them cannot but lead to the conclusion that they belonged to a period when the Buddhist influence was felt strongly in the south and when with the impetus given to the contact with the Yavanas (Greeks and Romans) there arose a school of art noted alike for the accuracy of its design and the chastity of its subject.

To much the same period must be attributed those thin small copper coins found in great numbers in and around Madura, which by their type and the legend imperfectly diciphèrable on a few of them, must be assigned a Roman origin. Though there have been finds of aurei and dinarii in many parts of South Inia, nowhere so far as we know, except in Madura and Ceylon, are these small copper pieces to be met with. Moreover it is noteworthy that, while the type of this thin copper coinage is distinct from that of the Roman Imperial coins discovered among the South Indian finds, there is at the same time no corresponding currency in gold and silver answering to the insignificant-looking copper pieces. It is beleived therefore that these copper coins must have been minted locally to meet the exigencies of a colony of Roman merchants that had settled in or around Madura. It is fairly certain that Roman soldiers were employed as body guards by the Tamil kings and to keep the gates of the Fort of Madura. A force of Roman Cohorts was stationed on the Malabar Coast to protect their trade. The Romans are said to have built a temple to Augustus at *Muchiri*, and a colony of Yavana merchants had settled at a place called *Caveripaddinam* which was a great emporium of trade in the Eastern Coast. In such circumstances, it is no extravagant theory to advance, that these small coins must have been issued for use in a small settlement of foreign merchants that had been established near Madura, for facilitating the extensive trade with India that we know was carried on by them in the first centuries of the Christian era. Most of them bear on their obverse the head of the Emperor with a legend around, while the reverse bears a striking resemblance to the reverse of the coins of Constantine.

Only one copper coin of a different type was found and that, not at Madura but at Devipatnam, during a period of nearly twenty five years of coin-hunting in Southern India. The obverse of this specimen bears the head of a female figure, legend Europa Roma, while the reverse bears the figure of a she-wolf suckling, Romulus and Remus, the reputed founders of Rome. From its type and from the place where it was found, it is unlikely that it was issued out of a local mint, but must have been a stray copper piece that found its way to India during the period when the trade between this country and the Roman Empire was in a flourishing state.

We next come to a series, which unmistakably bear the impress of the Pandiyan mint, bearing as they do on their obverse the Pandiyan emblem of the single or double fish. On coins of this series are generally found engraved in Tamil the names or birudus of the monarch in whose time the coin was issued.

These names or titles are :—

Avanipa Sêgaran

Avanipêndiran

Kodaṇḍarāman

Sundara Pāṇḍiyan

Kachi Valangum Perumāḷ.

The legends Avanipasekharan and Avanipendiran, are comparable with titles assumed by Sundara Pandiya as 'Conqueror of the world'. The coins bearing these legends were probably issued by a Pandya King named Avanipasegaran Srivallabha mentioned in an inscription on a rock south of the Rock Cut Jaina Temple at Sittannavasal in the Puducotta

State. The legend on the coin has been read as Avanipasekharan golaga but it is capable of being read also as 'Avanipasekharan Cholah' and it is not improbable that in the perennial conflict between the Pandyas and the Cholas, a Chola king secured a signal victory over the Pandyas and to mark the event issued coins with the Pandyan crest which by right of conquest he became entitled to use.

The legend '*Kodandaraman,*' may perhaps refer to Sundara Pandiya Jatvarman who in the Srirangam and Jambukeswaram inscriptions had it recorded that he was a second Rama in plundering Ceylon. 'Sri Kodandaraman' was a son of the Chola king Parantaka I who in the early part of the tenth century, claims to have defeated the Pandya king Rajasimha and slew "in an instant, at the head of a battle, an immense army despatched by the Lord of Lanka." If Chola inscriptions speak true he also invaded Ceylon. And the suggestion is here hazarded that Parantaka's son was probably left to govern the vanquished Pandya's country and the coins were issued to commemorate this remarkable event in Parantaka's reign. It was certainly the practice in those times in South India to issue coins or medals to mark a notable achievement of a monarch as illustrated by the legend 'Kachi Valangum Perumal,' literally meaning the King who gave back Conjiveram, commemorating a remarkable act of generosity even in Sundara Pandiya's age. The monarch, who conquered the Chola country generously restored it to the Chola king. These coins are of at least four varieties and some of them have the Tamil syllable "Su" on the obverse thus giving us a clue also to the name (Sundara Pandya) of the king who issued them.

The legend of Sundara Pandiya occurs in such a large number and variety of coins that it is hopeless to identify them with the reign of any particular monarch, though it may be fairly assumed that issues of Sundara Pandiya bearing the fish mark, were anterior to the period when Lankapura Dandanada according to the Mahavanso ordered that the Kahapana of Parakramabahu should be current in the Pandiyan Kingdom. For after this edict, the obverse on the Pandiyan coins seems to have almost always become the figure of a Rakshasa or King the rudely executed figure familiar to collectors of Sinhalese coins. By the time of Raja Raja Chola the "Ceylon Man," as this characterestic figure is generally known to South Indian Numismatists, seems to have been quite a familiar figure on the obverse of the Chola coins. What led to the adoption of this device by Raja Raja, the greatest monarch of his age, in supersession of the usual emblems found on Chola seals and coins of certain date, *viz.* the fish, bow and the tiger, it is not possible to definitely affirm. But it is enough here to note that the coins of the Pandiyan Kings continued to bear the fish mark alone till a particular period and it may not be amiss to place that period in the middle of the 13th century.

We next have to deal with a series, in which the place of the fish on the obverse is taken by the Chalukyan emblem of the boar. The legend on the reverse is usually 'Sundara Pandya.' The boar, from which all gold coins, have got the name of *Varaha*, was a favorite emblem with more than one dynasty and a familiar instance of this, is the appearance of the emblem on the Vijayanagara coins of Tirumalaroya. The Pandyan coins with the boar obverse, having always the legend 'Sundara' on their reverse, there is no clue whereby we can attribute them to any particular reign. The boar emblem was probably assumed on an intermarriage between the Chalukya and Pandiya kings or on a conquest of the Chalukyas by the Pandyas.

The legend 'Sundara' is not confined to coins bearing the fish and boar emblems alone, but is found on those bearing on the obverse, 'the Ceylon Man' or a standing figure with hands folded as in the act of worship of a Hindu devotee. The variety of coins, obviously belonging to different times, which bear the legened 'Sundara,' furnishes yet another argument in support of the position already advanced on the strength of the recitals in inscriptions, that there were many Sundara Pandyas holding sway in the Pandyan country.

The coins of Vira Pandya also bear the figure of the "Ceylon Man" on their obverse. This Vira Pandya evidently ruled after the 1st war of the Pandyan succession and after the edict issued by Lankapura Daṇḍanāda that Parākrama Bahu's Kahapana which bore the figure of the "Ceylon Man" should be used throughout the conquered country. It is only natural that out of respect to the power that was instrumental in restoring Vira Pandya's father to the throne, he should try to compliment his benefactors by using the device of the 'Ceylon Man' on Pandyan coins.

Coins with the legends, Būtala Vīran, Ellām-talayānān, Kaliyuga Rāma, Chōṇādu-Koṇḍān, Chērakula Rāman, also bear on their obverse the same device, 'the Ceylon Man.' These legends do not indicate any particular sovereign in whose reign the coin bearing each legend was issued, but merely the title each sovereign assumed by reason of the exploit he belived he had achieved. Thus 'Būtala Viran,' and Ellām-talayānān signify that the monarchs who assumed those titles, believed themselves to have been the only supreme warriors on the face of the earth or became the lord of all the mundane rulers. The coins of Ellām-talayānān have on some of them the syllable 'Su' probably indicating the name Sundara Pandya.

'Chōṇāḍu Koṇḍan', conqueror of the Chola country commemorates perhaps, a victory gained by a Pandya King in the never ceasing feuds between the two great Tamil Kingdoms.

"Kaliyugarāman and Chērakularāman" point possibly to the same facts as those recorded in the Srirangam inscription or to a second invasion of Ceylon, by the allied armies

7

of the Pandyas and Cheras. But a Māravarman Tirunelvēli Perumāḷ Vira Pandya has inscriptions of his in the Ramnad and Tinnevelly Districts and the lithic records in the latter District mention coins known as those of Kaliyugarāman. The coins bearing this legend have therefore to be attributed to one of the later Pandyas who probably ruled in the 15th century. 'Kulasekhara' might stand for one of the many kings of that name who, associated almost always with a Sundara Pandyan, ruled over the Pandyan country.

The coins found in Madura are generally of a different type from those which are found in the Tinnevelly District The latter are thicker in size, of a bolder type and invariably bear on the obverse the figure of 'the Ceylon Man.' Most of these have no legend imprinted on them, but have various devices of Gods and demigods from the Hindu Pantheon, associated along with a battle axe, features wholly unfamiliar in the Madura Pandyan coins. The legends that they bear are, Sundara Pandya, Kulasēkhara Pandya or Vira Pandya, names which occur in the inscription of the later Pandyas in the Tinnevelly District.

Notwithstanding this dissimilarity between the two types of coins, even the casual observer can detect a family resemblance between them and there can be no doubt whatever, that the coins were issued by the scions of the ancient line who after their real power was lost retained still the vestage of sovereignty in the limited territory acknowledging their sway.

The next variety of Madura coins assignable to the Pandyan Kingdom are those with the legends :—

Samarakōlākalan.

Kōnērirāyan

Bhuvanēka Vīran

The coins with the legend Samarakōlāhalan are of various types, the most ordinary of which is that with the figure on the obverse of a *Garuda* (the anthropoid kite) now treading on a fish, now holding a *Vimâna*, possibly the representation of the *Vimâna* which was covered with gold at Srirangam by a great ancestor Jatavarman Sundara Pandya. The traditional lists have a Samarakōlāhalan, but the date of that king must be much earlier than the period to which the coins in question must be attributed. During the period of these later Pandya Kings the Nayaka Viceroys of Vijayanagar were practically the rulers of the Madura country and the dominion of the Pandyan must have been very similar to that of one of the big Zemindars of modern times. Yet the Pandyan was allowed to issue his own money. A Pandyan king named Tribhuvana Chakravarthi Konerinmai-Kòndan is responsible for an inscription in the South Arcot district and registers by it an endowment for celebrating a festival called 'Buvanēkaviran Sandi.' And an inscription on the Ekâmbaranâtha temple in Conjiveram is said to have been made under the direction of a Bhuvanēka Vīran Samarakōlākalan dated A.D. 1469. The Konerinmai Kondan above referred to was probably the successor of this Samarakolakalan, and thus we have some authentic information of the sovereigns who probably issued the coins with these legends which abound in such large variety and number in the Southern Districts. The rule of the Nayaka was probably in the name of the titular Pandyan king and it is not unlikely that the conis were issued by the Naicks themselves in the name of the Pandyas, as in a later age the British East India Company struck coins with the effigy of Vishnu or in the name of Shah Alum.

The coins with the legend Koneriroyan have on their obverse the figure of a bull, and are very similar in type to the coins of the Vijayanagar dynasty. The title Bhuvanēka Vīran, 'literally the only warrior in the whole world' is very much like the title Bhutala Viran and inscriptions of the sixteenth century of kings with the title Bhutala Vira were discovered near Kanyakumari. With the type of coins just noticed comes to an end the list of Pandyan coins discovered up to date. Coins of a later time, issued during the Nayaka rule, bearing the names of Visvanada and his successors, sometimes also having the name of the presiding deity of the Madura Temple or the name of the town itself in Tamil and Telugu, occur in large numbers but they bear upon Pandyan history if at all, in a very remote manner and therefore are omitted from consideration. From the brief survey made of the coins that may be attributed with a fair amount of certainty to the Pandyan kings, it is found that except the very old coins issued possibly during the first centuries of the Christian era, when Buddhism was the state religion in the south as it was in the north, the coins unearthed till now belong to the period between the 9th and 14th centuries A.D.

THE KURAL.

BY

THE REV. DR. J. LAZARUS.

BY way of introduction it may be stated at the outset that the *Kural* is a Tamil poem on ethical subjects, held in the highest estimation by the Tamil people. No less than twelve commentaries have been written on this work by men representing different religious sects of Hinduism: the one written by the Brahman Parimêlaḷagar* being the most popular. The text itself is simple and readily yields its meaning to the diligent student. But as there is a "pleasure in poetic pains which only poets know," so in this matchless piece of poetic effort, there are depths of thought and heights of moral excellence which can only be perceived by those endowed with a sense for the true and the beautiful in life.

* [Parimelalagar is now-a-days considered as a Brahman, because he was a Sanskrit scholar, and a native of Conjiveram as the Thondamandala-Chadagam—a work scarcely of any value for historical purposes—would have it. But according to the traditional account Kadayam was his birth place and Pungavar-nattam his residence, where he spent the major portion of his life. Both these villages are in the district of Tinnevelly; the former situated on the bank of the Thambraparni to the west of Tinnevelly and the latter in *Karisal-Kadu* (black cotton-soil) to the north of Tinnevelly. A wealthy and munificent land-lord of the village Pungavar-nattam by name Veli-kanda Nadar was his patron. Parimelalagar himself was of the same caste as his patron—a Santar, and belonged to the *Gurukkal* family of the community. The site of his house is still discernible in the northernmost portion of the village. He was named *Parimelalagar* after the God-Siva of

Though universally known and frequently quoted, the *Kural* is not studied as intensely as it ought to be by the Tamil people. A few foreigners, however, have bestowed on its study a considerable amount of labour, time and thought. Among Frenchmen M. Ariel, among Italians Father Beschi, the greatest European Tamil scholar, among Germans Dr. Graul and among Englishmen Ellis, Drew, Robinson and Pope, have rendered valuable service by publishing partial or complete translations of the *Kural* and thus introducing it to

---

Madura who, according to the *Stala-purana*, appeared on horse-back as an Arabian horse-trader to save Manikkavacagar from the oppression of his king, the Pandya Arimardhana. (Alagar, Chockar, and Sundarar are but synonymous, meaning "the graceful," and *pari-mel.* "mounted *on horse*.") Parimelalagar was by religion a Saivite and the date of this able commentator of the *Kural* is about the 15th century A. D. and from his commentary we have to infer, he came after the great Nachchinarkkiniyar.

Parimelalagar had a son by name Kumarasami Gurukkal, who was also a poet and a scholar and has left behind him a work "Adiramayanam"—an allegorical treatise composed in verse. It is still preserved in cadjan leaves under the custody of one of the surviving descendants of the ancient and famous Veli-kanda Nadar. A clear and remarkable account of the descent of Parimelalagar the Editor chanced to gather from an old lady who according to her own account was the last descendant of Parimelalagar. This good old lady was living some 15 years ago at Iral a petty but flourishing village of the Santar community near Ettaiyapuram and not far from the said Punguvar-nattam. She was then about 90 years old, and although she had lost her sight, possessed a clear head and a noble heart. She became a widow while quite young and had no issue. She was held in great esteem by the villagers on account of her old age and virtuous character, besides her being a member of the *Gurukkal* family. With her the noble line of Parimelalagar terminates. To the information as to the existence of this old lady at Iral, the Editor owes his sincere thanks to the villagers of Pungavar-nattam. Branches of this *Gurukkal* family are at present found at Iral, Kadayam, Padukkapattu (near Kulasekhara Pattinam) Kachchina-vilai (near Alwar-tirunagari) and in some of the villages of Nanjil-Nadu (South Travancore). The members of this family invariably bear the title of "Aiya" or "Aiyar." This is a hereditary title owned, from time immemorial, by the community to which the great Parimelalagar belonged. Perhaps this has led the modern literary world as well as the late talented Bishop, Dr. Caldwell, to shift Parimelalagar from the Santar (சாண்றார்) community and place him in a Brahman environment.—*Editor T. A.*]

the learned public of Europe. Mr. Drew carried his translation to the end of the 63rd chapter, and the writer of this paper may be pardoned for adding that he was the first to publish a prose rendering of the remaining seventy chapters. The late Dr. Bower was quite familiar with the poet, but unfortunately he did not commit to writing the results of his critical, and life-long study of this great work. In his valuable Dravidian Comparative Grammar the late lamented Bishop Caldwell refers particularly to the *Kural* as the most ancient extant Tamil work and fixes the date of its composition at a period previous to the ninth century. This conjecture, however, has since been indisputably proved to be incorrect by Scholars who have investigated the subject with the light of literature and epigraphy. The late Professor Sundaram Pillai and Kanakasabai Pillai and Mr. S Krishnaswamy Aiyengar, M.A., M.R.A.S., have shown that Tiruvalluvar flourished in the Tamil Augustan Age, *i.e.*, in the first or the early year of the second century. The *Kural* is quoted in the Epics whose dates have been ascertained by internal evidence and contemporaneous history to have been in the second century.

With these introductory remarks, we may proceed to consider more fully the authorship, style and subject-matter of the work before us. Very little is known regarding the author of the *Kural*. His very name has not been handed down to posterity. From time immemorial he has been described as Tiruvalluvar, the sacred Pariah priest. The Pariahs are divided into eighteen tribes, at the head of which stands the Valluvan. He is their priest, soothsayer and doctor. Unlike the hut of the Pariah, the Valluvan's house is quite close to, if not on the very border of or just within, the 'village' proper and not in the *cheri* itself. He wears a thread like the twice-born. His services as a doctor and astrologer are in great demand among the higher castes, who treat him with respect and receive him into their houses. With reading and writing, he is more or less familiar, while he repeats by rote a great deal of current learning and common *mantras*. His general appearance is so neat that even a practised eye fails to see the Pariah in him. To this tribe then did the author of the *Kural* belong. And twenty centuries ago when the caste lines of demarcation were not so rigidly drawn as they are now, Tiruvalluvar must have enjoyed greater facilities for education, and more familiar intercourse with peoples of other classes, than is the case at present with his down-trodden castemen. A later tradition, however, makes the poet a son of a Brahman father and a Pariah mother,—evidently a foolish attempt to improve on the humble though purer ancestry of the Tamil bard. The words *Adi Bagavan* occur in the first distich of the Kural as an epithet of the Deity; and though the tradition would make it appear that *Adi* was the mother and *Bagavan* the father of the poet, it has utterly failed to alter the descriptive name of the poet, which still continues to be Valluvar.

The poet lived at St. Thomè or Mylapur, the southern suburb of Madras, and earned his livelihood as a weaver. How a Valluvan could take to working at the loom, is to us somewhat surprising. And surprising as this may be, it is still more surprising how a Valluvan weaver could win the hand of a Vellala maid of Cāvripauk. But so it was two thousand years ago. The poet is also said to have enjoyed the friendship and patronage of one Elasingan, a wealthy merchant of St. Thomè who belonged to the *Karaya* or *Parava* community, owned vessels and had trade with foreign countries. With his wife Vāsuki, therefore, the poet seems to have spent the greater portion of his life in this 'town of peacocks,' as the name Mylapore signifies, and gathered the materials for his immortal work, having probably as his contemporaries the Pandiyan Ugra-peru-valudi, Chancellor of the third acadamy in Madura and the Roman Emperor Claudius I, conqueror of Britain.*

* When Tiruvalluvar submitted his *Kural* to the Sangam Critics, the reigning sovereign in Madura was Ugra-Pandiyan, victor over the "Big Forest Fort" *(Kana-per-epil)* of Vengai-Marban. Avvai, who is claimed

But whence did the poet gather his materials? This is an important question and no less interesting. The most natural source must have been the vast literature of the Sangam period. And life in his time must, of course, have afforded his genius ample food for thought and reflection. Not far from his village was the Chola Kingdom invariably in alliance with the Pandyâs of the south. The follies and

as the sister of Valluvar and who was one of the three celebrities of the time—the other two being Kapilar and Paranar—has sung the praise of this Pandiyan and his two friends, the Cholan Perunarkilli and Cheran Mavenko. Both Kapilar and Paranar of the '*Great trio*' and another poet of no less fame known by the name of Perumkuntur-Kilar, have sung the praise of Vaiyaviko-perun-Pegan, a chief of the Vellala caste, whose daughter was given in marriage to Cheral-Athan—Chelva-kadumko, whom Kapilar has sung in the VIIth section of the "Ten Tens," and whose son Cheral-Athan-Vana-varamban became the son-in-law of Karikala I. Another king sung by Paranar and Perumkuntur-kilar is Cholan Ilanjed-chenni, father of Karikala I. From this we may infer that the contemporary kings of Pandiyan Ugra-peru-Valudi *alias* Ugra-Pandiyan were the Cholas—Perunarkilli and Ilanjed-chenni (brothers elder and younger respectively as the name suggests), and the Cheras—Mavenko and Chelva-kadumko (probably brothers) and the Count Perum-Pegan.

From the "Epic of the Anklet," we learn that, in the beginning of the 2nd century A. D., the reigning kings of the three Tamil Kingdoms were Pandiyan Nedum-cheliyan, Cholan Nedumudi-killi and Cheran Chenkuttuvan—the contemporaries of the Ceylon King Gajabahu I. Chenkuttuvan was a prominent figure of the day; he was the son of Cheral-Athan Vanavaramban above referred to and Nedu-mundi-killi (son of Karikala I) was his maternal uncle. Pandiyan Nedumcheliyan, the then ruling king of Madura, is known by the epithet the "Conqueror of the Aryan Army," thus distinguishing him from his predecessor of the same name, the "Hero of Alanganam." We find no mention in the "Epic of the Anklet" or its sequel "The Jewel Belt" regarding the existence of the academy at the time, nor do we find any Sangam-poet singing the glories of this "Conqueror of the Aryan Army." And we know Avvai and Kapilar have already passed away from the scene. Mr. S. Krishnaswamy Aiyangar, M A., in his learned article, "The Augustian Age of Tamil Literature," is inclined to think that the Pandyan Ugra-peru-Valudi was "no other than the ill-starred Pandyan Nedum-Cheliyan of the "Epic of the Anklet;" and the late Kanakasabhai Pillai, the learned author of the "Tamils 1800 Years Ago" places Ugra-Pandiyan as the third in succession after the Nedum-Cheliyan referred to in the Epic. Their conclusions, we fear, are not sufficiently vices of the Kings, the early training and education of the Princes, the intrigues of their courts, the varied gifts and tactics of the Ministers, the frequent wars which laid the states in ruins, the contests of warriors who combated with the courage and skill of gladiators, the frequency of famines and epidemics, could not but have filled the poet's mind with anxious thoughts regarding royal rectitude and the well-being of kingdoms. The *Kural* also bears testimony to the fact that the 'worker at the loom' was a close observer of life in its more familiar and humbler walks. The ascetic and the house-holder, the gambler and the drunkard, the farmer and the idler, the wedded husband and the unwedded lover, the devoted wife and the mercenary prostitute, the host and the guest, and parents and children do not escape the activity of his mind or the keenness of his eyes. Even nature, animate as well as inanimate, is laid under contribution. The roaring sea of St. Thomé beating with its creamy surf on the palm-grown shore, the hills and lakes, the brooks and rivers, the *topes* and groves in his neighbourhood, the flowers and herbs,

---

warranted by facts. We have noted above that Ugra-peru-Valudi was a contemporary of Perunar-Killi and Ilanjed-Chenni and thus an ancestor of the "ill-starred" Pandiyan Nedum-Cheliyan of the 'Epic of the Anklet,' who ordered the execution of the innocent Kovalan.

Chenkuttuvan is said to have reigned 50 years and his date falls between A. D. 95 and 145. He was the grandson (daughter's son) of Karikala the Great, whose age is fixed as 50 to 90 A. D. Thus the age of Ilanjed-Chenni, father of Karikala, and his contemporary Ugra-peru-Valudi should probably be fixed between 30 and 50 A. D. This is *the* age of the *Kural*, when our Valluvar, the Prince of Moralists, produced it to the Professors of the last Academy presided by Ugra-Pandiyan. This Ugra Pandiyan should either be identified with Nedum Cheliyan of the Alanganum fame, 'who was far and near terror to his enemies,' or, be his immediate successor. For we learn from the Sangam works that Cheran Mantharam Cheral Irumporai, who engaged in a war with Perunar-killi, was captured by this Nepoleon of the Ancient Madura and subsequently escaped. We have already pointed out that Perunar-killi, and Ugra Peruvaludi were contemporaries and friends. Mr. Kanakasabhai Pillai is far from correct in placing these potentates after Cheran Chenkuthuvan, contemporary of Gajabahu I of Ceylon, in his "Tamils 1800 Years Ago." *Ed. T. A.*]

the plants and shrubs, with the birds and animals of his country, the poet summons to his aid as he clothes moral 'dry bones' with life and beauty.

It is most likely that Tiruvalluvar with his active mind ever in quest of knowledge and bent on discerning truth from error, must have visited the third and last surviving University or College of Madura, and witnessed the hair-splitting controversies of the proud arbiters of learning in that ancient seat of Shen-Tamil. The rival schools of religion and philosophy which were in his time fast developing into rival sects, the spread of Buddhism and the decline of Jainism, the unsuitability of the Vedic and Brahmanic cult to the simple tastes of the Dravidian farmer, the moral worthlessness of rites and ceremonies,—these the poet had carefully scrutinized and found utterly useless for the system he was daily elaborating in his humble cottage.

It is often urged, and with considerable force, that at least for the purer moral sentiments of the *Kural*, the poet is indebted to Christianity. "We may fairly picture him," writes Dr. Pope, the latest advocate of this theory, "walking along the sea-shore with the Christian teachers, and imbibing Christian ideas, tinged with the peculiarities of the Alexandrian School, and day by day working them into his own wonderful *Kural*." But the *Kural* betrays no traces of distinctively Christian ideas or ethics such as may be ascribed to Christ or His Apostles alone. None of the ten epithets by which the Deity is described in the opening chapter of the *Kural* have the remotest connection with Christ or God, that is to say, as they are designated in the Bible. The chapter on Killing deals exclusively with the literal taking away of life. That on Love is quite different from the Apostle's eulogium in 1 Cor. xiii. Of course here and there, there are similarities of expression, nay even identical moral sentiments, but this is quite natural; for human nature is the same everywhere, and even oceans cannot separate kindred souls or moral instincts. Of one thing, however, we may be certain. In his daily intercourse with the Christians of Mylapore, which is quite probable, the poet must have observed the superior sanctity and attractiveness of the Christian home, which may have contributed in no small degree to the beautiful picture he has given us of a Tamil family.

When the work was completed the poet repaired, we are told, to Madura to secure for it the *imprimatur* of the College of Pandits there. It is said that at first the haughty professors, refused to review it. The author thereupon requested permission to place it on their 'divine seat' which was then afloat in a tank. The request was granted. But the seat immediately contracted itself to the size of the book and threw the professors into the tank. Shorn of all figure, the account means, that, though it was far from easy for the humble poet to get his work acknowledged by the southern luminaries as one of intrinsic merit, his ultimate triumph was complete.

The poet's life was a poem in itself. The concurrent voice of various traditions bears testimony to the happy and exemplary life he led with his beloved Vāsuki. She it was who had sat for the poet's portrait of the ideal wife. A pattern of perfect obedience and devoted virtue, she had never during her whole married life, questioned her lord's command. The night on which she died, the poet was heard to utter the following pathetic lines:

> "O thou loving one, O sweet'ner of my food,
> O wife who ne'er transgressed my word,
> Who did'st chafe my feet, rising first and sleeping last,
> O when will these eyes know sleep again!"

Vāsuki's death affected the sage so deeply that he soon secluded himself from society and devoted the rest of his life to religious contemplation. At his death, his body was, according to his expressed desire, exposed in the open air outside the town to be devoured by crows.

"Though dead he yet speaketh." To think is to live; and he by whom the reality and responsibility of life on earth was thought out in all its manifold bearings and aspects, still lives in the loving memory of millions. The despised Pariah has been raised to the highest pinnacle to which in the opinion of Hindus mortal man can rise: the Valluvan has become a god: he is regarded as an incarnation of Brahma. Brahman and Non-Brahman alike raise their hands in devout worship to this 'divine teacher.' Twenty centuries have not diminished the weight of his authority or the vitality of his utterances. He lives, and his fame will increase with the flight of time; and so long as men continue to revere the true and the good so long will the words of the poet continue to inspire them, and gain him a seat with the great teachers of the world.

The *Kural* then is the work which this great teacher has bequeathed to posterity. Like its author, the work too is nameless. The name by which it is known, is simply the name of the metre in which it is composed. Several Tamil poets have since followed our poet's example, and named their works after their respective metres. The word *Kural* means *short*. The root is *Kur*, a purely Tamil primitive. But it has its cognates in Sanskrit and other Aryan languages, and is one of the many distinctively Tamil roots which unmistakably prove the hoary antiquity of the language and its intimate connection with some pre-Aryan tongue from which the Aryan, Semitic, and Tamilian families are generally held to have descended. But as applied to Tiruvalluvar's work, the term signifies a shortened form of the metre called *Venba*. For the *Venba* consists of four lines while the *Kural*, or *Kural-Venba*, as it is properly termed, consists but of two. And it is quite probable that the poet's genius invented this couplet form as being the best fitted to convey his thoughts in the briefest form to his countrymen. It approaches the Sanskrit *sloka*, but is capable of clothing a perfect syllogism. The first line of each *Kural* contains four feet, and the second, three. With the exception of the seventh or last foot, the others may consist of two or three metrical syllables. And thus by a most skilful combination of these two kinds of feet (for which western prosody has no generic names), involving an endless variety of accent—of spondees and iambuses, trochees and dactyls, and a corresponding variety of rhythm and pause, with a judicious introduction of rhyme and alliteration as well as a careful selection of soft and hard consonants,—the poet plays on his two-stringed harp with matchless power and grace, and adapts his notes to every mood of mind or emotion of heart he desires to awaken in our souls.

Both critic and commentator unite in saying that the object of the *Kural* is to enable men to live, that is to say, live in the truest and highest sense, reminding us, very feebly it may be, of the words of Jesus who says, "I came that they may have life and have it abundantly." And from the *Kural* itself it may be gathered that while modern science defines life as a struggle against death, Tiruvalluvar by anticipation defines it as a struggle against the "sevenfold births."

In carrying out this great purpose the poet naturally treads in the path of Indian philosophers, and undertakes to write on the well-known four great themes, *viz.*, Virtue, Wealth, Pleasure and Heaven. The last being beyond the pale of human knowledge and experience, he wisely omits; though incidentally he approaches it elsewhere with great yearning of soul.

The plan of the *Kural*, therefore, is briefly as follows: first an Introduction of four chapters, followed by thirty-four on *Virtue*, practised by both the domestic and the ascetic; seventy on *Wealth*, earned both by the state and citizen; with twenty-five on *Pleasure*, enjoyed by unwedded lovers ending in conjugal life; making in all 133 chapters. Each chapter contains ten couplets. Thus there are altogether 1,330 distiches in the *Kural*. The late Mr. Scott of Madura recently published an edition of it with a re-arrangement of the plan and what he considered to be the necessary emendations of the text. But time will soon shew that it was a futile attempt. The *Kural* cannot be improved nor its plan made more perfect. It is a perfect mosaic in itself. The slightest change in the size, shape or colour of a single stone would mar the beauty of the whole. "Complete in itself," to quote the words of Dr. Pope, "the sole work of its author, it has come down the stream of ages absolutely uninjured,—hardly a single various reading of any importance being found."

Before proceeding to consider the poet's treatment of each of these grand topics, we must dwell very briefly on the Introduction. The four chapters treat respectively of God, Rain, Virtue and Ascetics,—and form a fitting type of the whole. The very first couplet on God, which is also the first in the whole work, is characteristic of the man and marks him out as a shining monotheist in those dark ages.

> ' As all letters have A for their first,
> So the world has the Eternal God for its first."

Thus does the Valluvan begin his great work. In other words, the poet would join hands with Moses and say, "In the beginning God created the heaven and the earth." This is the nearest Indian parallel to Christian cosmogony. Rain finds a place in the Introduction, because then as now, it was indispensable to the well-being of mankind. The fact that eight out of ten distiches describe the evils of drought, indicates the frequency of famines even in the poet's days. The chapter on Virtue, or Righteousness in Scriptual language is well worth study. He says:—

> " To be spotless in mind is alone virtue,
> All else is evanescent show."
> That alone is pleasure which flows from virtue."

The poet defines virtue and vice thus:—

> " Virtue is what ought to be done,
> And vice what one ought to shun."

A careful perusal of the *Kural* will shew that in dealing with Virtue, Wealth and Pleasure. the poet takes up types of the greatest excellence in each department. The householder and the ascetic in the first, the king and the citizen in the next, and conjugal bliss in the last are selected as leading ideals in the treatment and development of each of these subjects. The headings of the twenty-three chapters devoted to the portrayal of domestic virtue form, as it were, the main features of an excellent portrait. The house-holder, married not to a child-wife but to a frugal woman who is a meet help to his consecrated life, rejoices in the careful training of his children, through loving whom he learns to love his neighbour, is hospitable, given to kindly speech, grateful for benefits received, strictly just and upright in all his dealings, moderate and self-restraining, decorous in behaviour, faithful unto his wife, forgiving and forbearing, avoiding envy, covetousness, evil-speaking, even profitless gossiping, dreading evil deeds, always placing duty supreme, giving to the poor and preserving his good name. I doubt very much if anything could be added to enhance the beauty of this picture, especially as each of these features undergoes further and still finer touches from the poet's pencil. Sir Alex. Grant states that "humility, charity and forgiveness of injuries are not described by Aristotle." But it is these very qualities which are so forcibly and frequently inculcated by this Tamil bard. It is only the pen of a Drummond that could adequately bring to light the hidden beauty of his chapter on Love. One or two extracts will suffice :—

> "He alone lives who loves."
>
> "Nothing can restrain love.
> The tiny tear will betray it."

To these may be added one from the chapter on Forbearance :

> "Forgiving trespasses is good always,
> Forgetting them hath even higher praise."

The substance of the first couplet in chapter on Giving is simply " "Tis more blessed to give than to receive."

Ascetics seem to have formed an important and revered class in the poet's days. For their guidance, therefore he lays down a special code, which might be called the higher virtue. In this section, certain virtues and observances are treated of. Taking away life and flesh-eating are condemned, while benevolence, veracity and the like are commended, Referring to veracity, the poet says that "falsehood may be regarded as truth, if it yields guiltless good." This is the only instance in which the moralist leaves the intuitional platform and takes his stand on utilitarian ground. At all events, he acted up to his light.

The Jains claim the poet as belonging to their sect, because of his restrictions against killing and flesh-eating. But this cannot justify their claim. In these restrictions, he is laying down the law for the ascetic, not the ordinary householder. Besides people were mostly vegetarians then, as they are now; probably much more so. The abhorrence of flesh-eating and the slaughter it involves is common even now among vegetarians. And the poet simply gives expressions to public opinion in this respect without necessarily attaching himself to the Jains or to their system of theology. And the only two allusions to be found in the *Kural*,—one to Indra and the other to Vishnu under the epithet Tirumal—could not have been acceptable to the Jains who disbelieved the myths alluded to. On the other hand, Tiruvalluvar seems to have been an eclectic philosopher, carefully discarding everything which had not a rational or moral basis. It is true he refers to Fate and Transmigration. But the former he regards in nearly the same light as Christian Providence, while the latter he seems to have accepted as a temporary solution of the problem of life. But as I have already remarked, escape from this "sea of seven-fold births" is the burden of his work.

We now come to Wealth, the second part of th *Kural*. The king with equipped state and the law-abiding citizen are the types in this section of the work. The moral courage with which the humble poet ventures to frame laws for the well-being of the Chēra, Chōla and Pandyan kingdoms is certainly wonderful. It reminds one of the Jewish prophets of old. The poet perceived that if he could lay down certain general principles the observance of which would be conducive to the material welfare of the state, their application to individuals and families would be apparent. And hence this section of the *Kural* is an exquisite poem on political economy, or the wealth of nations. It is on this section that the poet brings to bear his learning, his observation and his unerring judgment. In the seventy chapters of this part, a great variety of topics is treated of with the same force and beauty which characterize the former portion. Kingly greatness, learning, observation, good associations, deliberation, misplaced confidence, fortitude under affliction, power in speech and purity in deed, thought-reading, tact in society, are some of the qualities he enlarges upon as being essential ingredients in what might be called a public man. The essentials of a state are then dwelt upon. It is here that we have the poet's beautiful chapters on Friendship, both good and bad. One or two couplets may be quoted:

> "The friendship of the wise increases like the waxing moon;
> That of fools diminishes like the waning moon."
>
> "True friendship dwells, not in the sweet smiles of the face,
> But in the sincere smiles of the heart."
>
> "Seek to gain the friendship of the pure;
> But renounce even with a gift that of all others."

A whole chapter is devoted to conscientiousness. Here are a few epigrammatic quotions:

> "Food, clothing and the like are common to all;
> But conscientiousness is peculiar to the good."
>
> "The conscientious will rather lose their life for their conscience,
> Than lose their conscience for their life."

"The poor," said Christ, "ye have always with you." It was so indeed in Tiruvalluvar's times. He too, in last chapters, speaks of poverty and begging; the latter, however, he condemns. He says,

"Even thin gruel is ambrosia to him
Who has earned it by labour."

With reference to royal greatness he says,

"He is a lion among kings who possesses
An army, people, wealth, minister, friend and fort."

There are some beautiful verses or Fortitude. For example,

"He has no sorrow in sorrow,
Who seeks no pleasure in pleasure."

"Sorrow flees before him
Who can tickle trouble into joy.

Regarding sins of omission and commission, the following I think cannot be surpassed:

"He dies who does what is not meet;
He also dies who does not what is meet."

Indeed, such verses are so very numerous that it is difficult to make a selection. And translation is often a hopeless task. The words indeed may be rendered, and to a great extent, the sentiments also. But to reproduce the beauty, the rhythm and the terseness of a couplet is simply impossible. The translator must himself be a poet. As has been well remarked, each couplet is, as it were, "an apple of gold in a network of silver."

The third part of the *Kural*, that on Pleasure, has been much animadverted upon. Fifty years ago Mr. Drew said that it could not be translated without "exposing the translator to infamy." Public opinion, however, has greatly changed since that time. Dr. Graul has not only rendered it into German and Latin, but has said something in praise of its intrinsic excellence. The fact is, as I have already pointed out, the poet chooses types and ideals for the elucidation of his themes. When about to explain the nature of true pleasure, he perceives with the Christian poet that domestic felicity is the "only bliss that has survived the fall." Even the Apostle Paul could find no better analogy for the union of Christ and His Church than that of wedded love. Dr. Pope thinks "he will be regarded as having done good service" in translating it. It was one of the couplets in this part of the poem, referring to the two looks of a maid—the one which kills and the other which cures the looker—that led Dr. Graul to admire Tamil poetry and study the *Kural*.

At the same time it must not be forgotten that ancient writers were far less reserved in their style of writing on such subjects than is the case with modern authors; and that almost all eastern literature is, more or less, tainted with an excess of liberty in this particular. Still, it must be stated to the credit of the poet that this section is perfectly pure in its tendency, though its style is different from that of the other portions. It embodies no rules for conduct. On the contrary by a few scintilations of poetic fancy, it aims at giving the reader a vivid though distant glimpse of the perfect bliss of conjugal life. It consists mainly of soliloquies and dialogues, and embraces unwedded as well as wedded love for both forms of union were permitted in the poet's days. But of the twenty-five chapters, only eight are devoted to unwedded love—thus indicating the decided opinion of the poet who in the eighth chapter makes the unwedded union end in wedded love. A few couplets may be quoted in illustration of what has been said:

> "Ah, woe is me! my might that awed my foeman in the fight,
> By lustre of that beaming brow borne down lies broken now."

> "I look, but her eyes are on the ground the while;
> I look away and she looks on me with timid smile."

> "If it is not parting, speak to me; but if 'tis quick return,
> Speak to those who can survive till then."

> "Like the eye which sees not the pencil which paints it
> I cannot see my beloved's faults when I meet him."

But, it may be asked, may this portion be read by the young? I should say, no; no more than other eastern books, including even certain portions of the Old Testament, can be placed in their hands without injuring their immature minds.

We have thus cast a hasty glance at the contents of this remarkable work. It now remains to offer a few remarks on its general style and language. The *Kural* is composed in the purest Tamil. In about 12,000 words which the poet has employed to convey his thoughts, there are scarcely fifty of Sanskrit origin. He throws the purity of Bunyan's English completely into the shade. No known Tamil work can even approach the purity of the *Kural*. It is a standing rebuke to modern Tamil. Tiruvalluvar has clearly proved the richness melody and power of his mother-tongue. And while the composition of a master-piece like the *Kural* so many centuries ago demonstrates the great antiquity and careful culture of the Tamil language, it is sad to reflect on the condition to which this great vehicle of thought has degenerated in these days with neither poet to sing, nor moralist to teach,—especially when during this same period a new language—that of Great Britain—has arisen and developed into a perfect tongue and bids fair ere long to occupy the greater part of the globe.

Regarding the *Kural* as a whole, there is but one opinion as to its surpassing excellence. Both European and Indian have written in the highest praise of it. In a little work, usually attached to native editions of the *Kural*, and called the Garland of Tiruvalluvar, there are fifty-three verses attributed to the discomfited professors of the Madura *Sangam* or College in each of which every variety of hyperbole is exhausted by the author in his praise of the poem and the poet. The latter is called God, the first of poets, the divine poet, Brahma, Lakshmi's consort, etc.; while the former is termed the Triple Treatise, the Later Veda, the Word of God, the Word of

Truth, the Tamil Vedam, and the World's Book. One of these critics says of it that it is a semi-perforated mustard seed into which the poet has emptied the contents of the seven seas. He refers of course to its *multum in parvo* characteristic. Most of these critics also refer to the chapters as well as sections as these have come down to us. One of these verses discloses that the poet flourished in the reign of Ugra-peru-Valudi, a Pandyan king, whose date is to be sought in the beginning of our era.

A European estimate of this work cannot be out of place here. Dr. Barth in his "Religions of India" refers to it as that "admirable collection of stanzas in the Tamil language which is instinct with the purest and most elevated religious emotion." M. Ariel, the French translator, calls it "the master-piece of Tamil literature"; and adds, "that which above all is wonderful in the *Kural* is the fact that its author addresses himself, without regard to castes, people or beliefs, to the whole community of mankind; the fact that he formulates sovereign morality and absolute reason; that he proclaims in their very essence, in their eternal abstractedness, virtue and truth; that he presents, as it were, in one group, the highest laws of domestic and social life; that he is equally perfect in thought, in language, and in poetry, in the austere metaphysical contemplation of the great mysteries of the Divine nature, as in the easy and graceful analysis of the tenderest emotions of the heart." Yes, it is a wonderful work, second only to that other Eastern literature which has received the impress of the Divine mind. Tiruvalluvar seldom discusses; he speaks with authority; his utterances are all *ex cathedra.* All his appeals are to the human conscience straight and direct. In the Veda, in the Code of Manu, and in the great Epics, the chief aim is the exaltation of the Brahmin; in the *Kural*, it is the exaltation of *man* as such, the race as a whole. The very ideal of the perfect man which he presents, according to the light he has received from Him "who lighteth every man that cometh into the world," cannot fail to inspire men of any creed or clime with purer motives for conduct and nobler aspirations for life.

The one great defect of the *Kural*—and it is one which belongs to every unaided human effort—is its conception of God. It is true the poet does not speculate: but he oscillates between the personal and impersonal idea in the solitary chapter he devotes to the "praise of God." In one couplet he speaks of God as one devoid of desire and aversion, in another he gives Him eight attributes, while in a third he calls Him the destroyer of the five senses. It could not have been otherwise. The poet, though a giant in the moral world was after all a child in the spiritual, with his foot on its threshold "seeking the Lord if haply he might feel after Him and find Him." "'Tis Revelation alone satisfies all doubts." In the chapter on Renunciation, there is a remarkable verse in which the yearning soul seems to gain a glimpse of the faith by which the "just shall live." It runs thus:

"Cling to that which He to whom
Nought clings, hath bid thee cling,

And cling to that bond to free thyself
From every clinging thing."

In other words, the poet would say, "To get rid of sin, cling in faith to the Sinless One."

In conclusion, it is refreshing to think that a nation which has produced so great a man and so unique a work cannot be a hopeless, despicable race. The morality he preached could not have grown except on an essentially moral soil. To those therefore who labour for the salvation of the Tamil people, the *Kural* must be a work of peculiar, nay, intense interest. To move, to persuade, to convince the poet's countrymen, the popular reformer or preacher must be perfectly familiar with the *Kural*, so that from their own *vedam* they may be led to seek that ideal, perfect Man, whom not having seen but instinctively feeling after, the poet has sought to sketch in his immortal work, which, in the words of an ancient Tamil critic is.

> "Sweet to the thought, sweet to the ear,
> Sweet to the mouth, and which with tongue
> Right eloquent, Tiruvalluvar set forth,
> That we the way of good may know."

"Sage Valluvar, priest of thy lowly clan,
No tongue repeats, no speech reveals thy name;
Yet, all things changing, dieth not thy fame,
For thou art *bard of universal man*;

And still thy book above the waters wan,
Virtue, true Wealth, and Joy, and being's aim,
In sweetest mystic couplets doth proclaim,
Where winds sea-wafted palmy forests fan.

Haply undreamed of *visions* glad thine eyes
In realms beyond thy fabled *seven-fold birth,*
And clouds of darkness from thy spirit roll;
While lands far-off have heard with strange surprise
Faint echoes of thy song. Through all the earth
Men hail thee brother, seer of spotless soul."

A CHAPTER FROM THE KURAL.

BY

MR. J. M. NALLASAMY PILLAI, B.A., B.L.

NOBODY who has the least insight into the pages of the sacred *Kural* will fail to endorse the remark of the veteran Tamil scholar, Rev. Dr. G. U. Pope, that this is a work unparalleled in any language. The merits of the work are so apparent that even at its very birth, it received the highest encomiums of the proudest scholars of the day, the Paṇḍits of the far-famed Madura College or Sangam. The tradition that the author was of low birth only hightens the value of the appreciations thus showered on him. One of the Collegians compares it to the Veda, and another says, unlike the Veda, Tiruvaḷḷuvar's words do not lose their merit by anybody repeating them. One speaks of it as containing everything worth knowing, and another that there is nothing which is not contained in this work. One says that the words are sweeter than the Heavenly Ambrosia, and unlike the latter, can be partaken of by everybody. And as the poet utters these words even our own mouth begins to water. Another says they are sweet food to the mind, sweet to the ear and sweet to the tongue, and the great *panacea* for the ills of Karma. One compares it to the sun which dispelling the deep darkness of ignorance, makes the lotus of the heart bloom forth. Another compares it to the lamp dispelling our mental darkness, with the oil-can of *Dharma*, and wick of *Artha*, and ghee of *Kama*, words of fection—the flame, and the short metres—the lamp-stand. Its brevity, not bordering on unintelligibility or ambiguity as do most of the Sūtras in Sanskrit, its perfection of expression and style, its deepness are all matters taken up for praise by these learned Collegians. And what is more, the poet Kallāḍar brings out in his verse its most prominent character, its universality. People wrangle about this or that being the truth, and they range themselves into various schools, but all are agreed about the truth of the words uttered by Tiruvaḷḷuvar. And since his time, all religionists—Buddhists and Jains, Saivas and Vaishṇavas, have all claimed him as their own. And we need not enquire wherefrom he derived his truths. It is enough to acknowledge that it is perfection of Truth, if one can say so, a Perfect Ethical and Religious Code, a perfection of art and thought. Indeed, a close study of the work will bring out its perfect scientific basis and each part, and each chapter, and each verse is placed one after the other in a perfect chain of logical arrangement and argument. And may we hope that some ardent student of the *Kural* will work out from it a perfect theory of ethics, both private and international.

One more remark, and this will introduce us to the chapter of the book we have taken up for translation and elucidation. It is usually remarked, following the main divisions of the book into Dharma, Artha and Kāma அறம், பொருள், இன்பம் that the author has left out the discussion of the last Purushārtha or Mōksha, வீடு, on the ground that religion is a matter which will give room for difference and dispute. But is it true that there are no universal truths of religion and did our author leave them unsaid? His own contemporaries did not understand him as doing so, but have stated in their encomiums that he has explained all the four Purushārtams and that he has shown the path to *Mòkṣha*. And the Rev. Dr. Pope in his short paper on the Ethics of Kuraḷ holds that Tiruvaḷḷuvar bases his ethics on the grand truths of *Tripadàrtha*—Pathi, Pasu and Pāsa. In fact, his creed is not a godless creed like that of the Jains or Buddhists Our author's God is the 'First Cause and Lord' 'ஆதிபகவன்;' He is 'Intelligent,' 'வாலறிவன்'; He 'resides in the heart of his creatures' 'மலர்மிசையேகினான்;' He is 'Immaculate, Untainted by likes and dislikes;' 'வேண்டுதல் வேண்டாமையிலான்' He is the 'Lord of Lords' and 'King of Kings' 'இறைவன்;' He is 'Incomparable', 'தனக்குவமையில்லாதான்;' He is the 'Source of all Dharma and Beneficent, 'அறவாழி அந்தணன்;' He has eight attributes, 'எண்குணத்தான்' (*i. e.* Self-Dependent or Self-Possesed, the Pure, Self-Luminous, the All Knowing, the Ever-Free, the Beneficent, the Infinitely Powerful and Infinitely Blissful) and the Eternal Truth, மெய்ப்பொருள், and the Perfect and Good Being; 'செம்பொருள்.'* No amount of learning is of any good unless a man believes in the existence of God and worships His feet in all love and truth. And without such knowledge and such conduct, the mere attaining of ethical perfection is of no use (Vide St. 4 below.) The true way to get rid of our bonds is to reach the feet of the Ever-Free. And these bonds are not mere myths but they are caused by our own ignorance. And then, the chain of causation following *karma* into endless births and suffering is worked out, and the means or *Sâdana* required to get freed from these bonds are fully shown, and of all the means, the greatest *Sâdana* is to reach Him who is past all thought and speech; and unless this is done, it is useless to hope to get our cares destroyed. And as all these principles are fully explained in chapter XXXVI on மெய்யுணர்தல், "How to perceive Truth," we have translated the same below, adopting almost the language of Dr. G. W. Pope, together with the famous commentary of Parimēlalagar, with and some running notes, here and there.

HOW TO PERCEIVE TRUTH ?

That is, we know the Truth when we know the nature of Birth and Freedom (Mōksha) and the causes thereof, free

---

* Pandit Savariroyan derives 'Sivam' from 'செம்' and our Saint uses 'செம்பொருள்' very frequently.

from error and doubt. This the Sanskritists call *Tatvajnâna*. As this knowledge arises after desiring the desire of Him who has no desire, this chapter is placed in consequence after the chapter on 'துறவு', 'Sanyāsa.'

1. பொருளல் லவற்றைப் பொருளென் றுணரும்
மருளானா மாணாப் பிறப்பு.

The delusion whereby men deem that the truth which is not;
That is the cause of hapless birth.

(COMMENTARY.)

This delusion consists in believing such books and doctrines which hold that there is no rebirth, no fruits of both kinds of *karma* and that there is no God and such like, to be the true books and doctrines. This delusive belief is same as when one mistakes one thing for another, a block for a man, shell for silver. மருள். "delusion," மயக்கம், "error," அவிச்சை, "*Avidya* or ignorance," are all synonymous words. As it is only sorrow that is reaped in all the four kinds of birth as dēvas, men, animals and astrals, this couplet explains that birth is sorrowful and *avidya* or error is its cause.

2. இருணீங்கி யின்பம் பயக்கும் மருணீங்கி
மாசறு காட்சி யவர்க்கு.

Darkness departs, and rapture springs to men who see
The mystic vision pure, from all delusion free.

(COMMENTARY.)

இருள், darkness is hell. 'The mystic vision pure' is the supreme object of knowledge. By this couplet is explained that by freedom is meant *Niratisayananda* and the *Nimitta Kârana*, for this, the Supreme Being. (*In the next couplet it is stated that even this doubt is the cause of birth, and the means of getting rid of this doubt is also stated.*)

3. ஐயத்தினீங்கித் தெளிந்தார்க்கு வையத்தின்
வானம் நணிய துடைத்து.

When doubts disperse and clearness is gained,
Nearer is heaven than earth to sage's soul.

(COMMENTARY.)

Doubt (ஐயம்) is knowing a thing variously. That is doubting if there is or is not God and Karma and Rebirth and without definite belief in anything. This is the same as doubting a thing as water or a mirage, rope or a snake. As it is natural to every system to refute other doctrines and establish its own, the doubts arising from such a multitude of doctrines, those sages well practised in Yoga will remove, by their *Svânubhûti* or experience, and attain to real knowledge; and hence they are called ஐயத்தின் நீங்கித் தெளிந்தார். As they reach higher and higher *Yogic* experience, their attachment to the world grows less and less: hence the author's statement that "heaven is nearer," etc. By this couplet is explained that doubtful knowledge is a cause of birth.

4. ஐயுணர் வெய்தியக் கண்ணும் பயமின்றே
மெய்யுணர் வில்லா தவர்க்கு.

Five-fold perception gained, what benefits accrue
To them whose spirit lacks perception of the True?

(COMMENTARY.)

Five-fold perception is the *Manas*. By 'gained' is meant the controlling of the *manas* and concentrating of it in *Dârana*. As training of this alone is not sufficient, the author says there is no benefit, and he brings out by the 'உம்,' how difficult a feat even this attainment of *Dârana* is. By these two couplets the greatness of *Pathijnâna* is explained by pointing out that without this attainment, no *Moksha* is possible. (*And the nature of this Pathijnana, "the knowledge of the Lord," is the subject of the next couplet.*)

5. எப்பொருள் எத்தன்மைத் தாயினும் அப்பொருள்
மெய்ப்பொருள் காண்ப தறிவு.

Whatever thing, of whatsoever kind it be,
'Tis wisdom's part in each the real thing to see.

(COMMENTARY.)

That is, one must perceive the truth immanent in every thing, after getting rid of our ordinary notions of them. In the phrase "சேரச்சேரமான் பாலைக்கட்சேரய் மாந்தருஞ்சேர லிரும்பொறை," the words may mean ordinarily the name of king Chēramān of a particular description, etc., etc., etc.; but they may mean more particularly the *Tattvas* from earth to *Purusha.* When examined and rendered into their final causes, what finally remains is none of this cause and effect, but the Highest Truth, and His knowledge is the true knowledge. By this couplet, is explained the nature of this *true knowledge.*

NOTE.—This is one of the most oft-quoted couplets of Kural, and is put to more general uses than what is intended here. One has not to go far to discover the Supreme Being and know Him. He is in everything; but one must lose light of the apparent to gain the real. God is in the earth but the earth is not God; Gou is in water but water is not God, and so through every Tattva, and lastly, God is in the soul, but the soul is not God. When one has so learned to discriminate and distinguish, then only will he attain to *Patijnânam.* In the next three couplets, the *Sâdana,* "means," required for attaining this *Patijnânam* is given. And the first requisite is hearing or learning.

6. கற்றீண்டு மெய்ப்பொருள் கண்டார் தலைப்படுவர்
மற்றீண்டு வாரா நெறி.

Who learn and here the knowledge of the true obtain,
Shall find the path that cometh not again.

(COMMENTARY.)

By 'learn,' the author means learning from every body and at all times. By 'here,' the author brings out the greatness of human birth wherefrom alone one can attain *Moksha.* "The path that cometh not again" is the path to *Moksha.* The means or *Sâdanâ* for knowing The First Cause, the cause of one's attaining Moksha are of three kinds: they are கேள்வி, "Hearing or Study", விமரிசம், "Reflection," பாவனை, "Realising." This couplet explains "கேள்வி," Hearing or *Sravana.*

7. ஓர்த்துள்ள முள்ள துணரின் ஒருதலையாப்
பேர்த்துள்ள வேண்டா பிறப்பு.

The mind that knows with certitude what is and ponders well,
Its thoughts on birth again to other life need not to dwell.

(COMMENTARY.)

This explains "விமரிசம்" Reflection or *manana*.

8. பிறப்பென்னும் பேதைமைநீங்கச் சிறப்பென்னும்
செம்பொருள் காண்ப தறிவு.

When the folly of desiring birth departs, the soul can view
The *exalted* Home of The Good Being, this is wisdom true.

(COMMENTARY.)

Birth and ignorance, and Exalted Home and Truth are really related as effect and cause, they are given inversely in this couplet. Of the five faults, as ignorance is the cause of even the other faults, the author has stated this as *the* cause of birth. As *Mokshá* is higher than all other things, it is spoken of as the 'exalted.' The First Cause is spoken of as the 'Good Being,' inasmuch as He is eternal without birth and death, as all other things are too insignificant to taint Him by their contacts, and as He remains the same without change or taint at all time, though immanent in all things. Hence also, He is spoken of above as the 'True being (மெய்ப்பொருள்) and the Existent (உள்ளது.) The "viewing" is the soul losing its *mala* by constantly realising or practising (பாவித்தல்), *Bâvana* so that it may become one with God (ஒற்றுமையுற). As it is commonly held by all schools of people that the soul when it leaves the body becomes that which it fancied at the time (அதனால் யாதொன்று பாவிக்கப்பட்டது அஃது அதுவாய்த் தோன்றுமாதலால்) *i. e.*, is born assuming that body to which it yearned at the time of death,) and so, too, as it is necessary for people who aspire after Mōksha to contemplate on the Transcendent Being, so that their thoughts on birth may cease, there is no better means than this *Sadana* for practice beforehand always. Thus பாவனை, (*Bavana*) "Realising," is explained in this couplet.

9. சார்புணர்ந்து சார்பு கெடவொழுகின் மற்றழித்துச்
சார்தரா சார்தரு நோய்.

The true 'support' who knows—rejects 'supports' he sought before
Sorrow that clings shall cease and cling to him no more.

(COMMENTARY.)

'ஒழுக்கம்' 'conduct or practice' here means practice of *Yoga*. This Yoga is of eight kinds; Yama, Niyama, Asana, Prānāyāma, Pratyākāra, Dhārana, Dhyāna, and Samādhi. Their explanations are too long to be given here. See them in the books on Yoga. 'The sorrows that cling to us' are the fruits of *karma* which have yet to be experienced, which are the result of infinite *karma* performed in births dating from eternity, and which give rise to fruits already eaten in past births and in the present birth. "Shall cease and cling no more," as they will vanish before Yoga and Jnāna like darkness before light. This Jains call 'உவர்ப்பு.' As even good *karma* is the seed of birth, it is called a 'disease.' The author holds that births will cease when the Supreme is perceived by the above mentioned three means. When the births cease, what can all the ills do, as they cannot cling to these Jnānis well practised in Yoga, and there being no support, they will die. This is the purport of the stanza.

NOTE.—The word 'சார்பு' in the verse and 'பற்று' in the previous chapter mean a *support* or *hold*. The soul has two such supports, one in *Bandha* and one in *Moksha* and without such supports it cannot stand. This may be compared to a piece of iron held between two magnetic poles, one positive, and one negative, or better still to a fruit growing on a tree. The fruit is held up by the tree, so long and so long only, as it is raw and immature (undeveloped) but so soon as it is ripe, it reaches the ground (Force of gravity); fruit, as such, must be united to the tree or the ground. What happens is, as the fruit grows riper and riper, the sap of the tree does not rise up to the twig and the twig dies, and it falls off. So too as man rises higher, and his desire of the world decreases, and the bonds are sundered, he drops into the Feet of the Lord. "பாசங் கழன்றுற் பசவுக் கிடம் பதியாம்." The author of திருக்களிற்றுப்படியார் explains 'சார் புணர்வு' as *Dhyâna*, and 'சார்புகெட ஒழுகல்' as *Samâdhi*, the highest *Jnâna-Yôga* practices. In the next verse this *Pâsâtchaya*, "Ceasing of the bond," is further explained.

10. காமம் வெகுளி மயக்க மிவைமூன்றன்
    நாமங் கெடக்கெடு நோய்.

When lust and wrath and error's triple tyranny is o'er,
Their very names for aye extinct, their pain shall be no more.

(COMMENTARY.)

The eternal ignorance, *avidya*, the consequent *agankara*, the feeling of 'I' and 'mine', the hankering which desires this or that, the eternal desire of this or that object, and dislike or hate arising from unsatisfied desire, these five faults are enumerated by Sanskritists. The author enumerates only three, as 'Agankāra' can be brought under 'Avidyā,' and 'hankering' can be comprised under 'desire.' As these faults are burnt up before Jnāna-Yôga practices, like cotton before a wildfire, so the author speaks of the disappearance of the very names of these three faults. As those who do not commit these faults, will not commit good or bad *karma* caused by them, the author states accordingly in this verse that they suffer no pain therefrom. As a result of the attainment of True Knowledge, the ills of past births and of future births are destroyed, and thus these two verses find a place in these chapter. We learn from this also, that what remains to those who have perceived the Truth is the present body and ills attaching thereto.

THE GOLDEN RULE.*

[*Kural : Chapter XXXII*]

The good are resolved not to injure or hurt,
Though 'twould gain them that wealth which brings
[greatness on earth.

Nor will they return of the ill they receive,
Though a foe should inflict an undeserved pain.

If one should do hurt to an unprovoked foe,
He will never escape from the sorrow 'twill bring.

Would you punish the man who has injured your mind?
Oh, put him to shame by your kindness and love.

What good has he gained by his knowledge and skill,
If he strive not for others as much as himself?

No man should consent to inflict or permit
What he knows will give pain to his bitterest foe.

Of virtues the chief—to do nought that is mean,
Though the man may be bad and the time apropos.

Why do men e'er inflict upon others the pain
That experience teaches themselves to avoid?

If a man in the morning bring grief to his foe;
With the eve, uninvited, 'twill come to himself.

To give pain to another brings ten back again.
Would you guard you from grief? To another cause none.

---

* From the "Folk-Songs of Southern India" by Charles E. Gover. [1871.]

THE TAMILS IN THE EPIC AGE.

பாரதகாலமும் தமிழரும்.

BY

PANDIT M. RAGHAVA AIYANGAR Avl., *(Ramnad.)*

செந்தமிழறிஞர்கள் தமிழ்ச்சரித்திர நுட்பங்களைப் பலபடியாக இக்காலத்து ஆராய்ந்து வருகின்றனராயினும், அவ்வாராய்ச்சிகளிற் பெரும்பாலனவும் கடைச்சங்க நிகழ்ச்சியைப் பற்றியும் அதன் பிற்காலத்து நிகழ்ச்சியைப் பற்றியுமே அமைந்துள்ளன. இவற்றிற்கும் முற்பட்ட தமிழின் உண்மை நிலையைத் தெரிதற்குப் போதிய கருவிகள் இதுவரை கிடைத்தில. "இறையனார் களவியலுரை" முதலியவற்றில் முற்காலத்திருந்த தலையிடைச் சங்கங்களைப் பற்றிச் சிற்சில செய்திகள் தெரியவரினும், அம்மட்டோடு போதுமென அமையாது, மேலும் அறிதற்கு நம்மனம் அவாவுகின்றது. யாழ்பாணத்து ஸ்ரீமத். முத்துத்தம்பிப்பிள்ளையவர்கள் சொல்லுமாறு:—"காலதேசங்களாற் சேய்மைக்கட்பட்ட பொருளை ஆராய்தலும் துணிதலும் அரிய கருமமாயினும் அப்பொருளை அறிதற்கே மனம் அவாவுவதாகும். ஐயாயிரம் பதினாயிரம் வருஷங்களுக்கு முற்பட்ட விஷயங்களை ஆராய்ந்து துணியுமிடத்து உளதாகும் ஆனந்தத்திற்கு உவமை பிறிதொன்று மில்லை. தேசத்தாற் சேய்மைக்கட்பட்ட சூரியாதி கிரகங்களின் தன்மைகளை ஒருவாறு யந்திரங்களால் அறிதலும் துணிதலுங் கூடும். இறந்த காலமென்னும் பரந்த திரையிட்டு மறைந்துபோய்ச் சேய்

மைப்பட்ட விஷயங்களை அத்திரை நீக்கிக் காண்டற்கோ ஒரு கருவியை யாயினும் யந்திரத்தை யாயினும் காண்கிலம். ஆயினும் அச்செய்மைக்கு அண்மைக்கட் செய்யப்பட்ட நூல்களைக் கருவியாகக்கொண்டு, அத்திரையை ஒருவாறு துருவி நோக்குதல் கூடும்." அங்ஙனம் நோக்கிக் கண்டதே மேல்வரும் விஷயமாம்.

ஆதியில் மூன்று சங்கங்க ளிருந்தன என்னும் பிரபலச் செய்தியில் நவீனர் சிலர் ஐயுறுகின்றனர். அவ்வையத்திற்கு அவர் கூறுங் காரணங்களில் முக்கியமானது, பழைய நூல்களிற் சங்கத்தைப் பற்றிப் பிரஸ்தாப மில்லை என்பதே. சிறிது நுணுகி யாராய்ந்தால் இக்கூற்றுப் பொருத்த முடையதன் றென்பது புலப்படும். இடைச்சங்கம் இருந்தாருள் நிலந்தரு திருவிற் பாண்டியன் என்பான் ஒருவனென்பது முன்னூல்களிற் காணப்படுகின்றது. இவனே தொல்காப்பியம் புலப்படுத்தினோன். இதனை "நிலந் தரு திருவிற் பாண்டியன் அவையத்து" எனவரும் அவ்விலக்கண நூற் பாயிரத்தால் அறியலாம். இவனைப்பற்றிக் கடைச்சங்கத்தாராகிய மாங்குடி மருதனார், மதுரைக்காஞ்சியில் "தொல்லாணை நல்லாசிரியர் புணர் கூட்டுண்ட புகழ்சால் சிறப்பின், நிலந்தரு திருவின் நெடியோன்" எனப் புகழ்ந்திருக்கின்றனர். இதனுள், சங்கமென்னும் வடசொல்லாற் பெயர் கூறுமற் போயினும், அப் பாண்டியன், நல்லிசைப்புலவர் பலரைக்கொண்டு செந்தமிழ் ஆராய்ச்சி செய்தான் என்பது "புணர் கூட்டுண்ட" என்பதனால் விளக்கமாம். அன்றியும், பண்டைத் தமிழ் வேந்தரிடம் தமிழ்ப் புலவர் பேரவை எக்காலத்துமிருந்து செந்தமிழாராய்ச்சி செய்து வந்த தென்பதிலும், அதுவே "சங்கம்" என்னும் பெயராற் பிற்காலத்து அழைக்கப்பட்ட தென்பதிலும் அதிசயிக்கத் தக்க தொன்று மில்லை. ஆதலால் முச்சங்கங்களைப் பற்றிய செய்தி முழுதையும் நவீனர் சிலர் ஐயுறுவது பொருந்தாதாம்.

இனி, அம் முச்சங்கங்களுள் தலைச்சங்கச் செய்திகளாக வழங்குவனவற்றில், முரஞ்சியூர் முடிநாகர் என்பவர், அச்சங்கமிருந்

தாருள் ஒருவரென்று 'இறையனார் களவியலுரை' முதலியவற்றிற் சொல்லப்படுகின்றது. இவரைப் போலவே, சிவபிரான், முருகவேள், அகத்தியனார் முதலியோரும் அச்சங்கத்தவராகக் கூறப்படினும், அவர்கள் தெய்வங்களாகவும் தெய்வத்தன்மையுடையோராகவும் இருத்தலால், அவரைப் பற்றிய ஆராய்ச்சி ஈண்டு நிகழ்த்தற்குரிய தன்று. ஆனால், முடிநாகர் என்பார் புதியராய் நிற்றலின், அவர் யாவர்? எக்காலத்தவர்? எவ்வகையினர்? என்பன விஷயங்களை முதலில் ஆராய்ந்து, அவர் மூலமாகப் பாரதகாலத்துத் தமிழ்மக்கள் யாவரென்று பின்னர் ஆராய்வாம்.

பழைய புலவரது வரலாறுகள் சிலவற்றை ஆராய்வதற்குக் கடைச்சங்க காலத்தில் இயற்றப்பட்டும் தொகுக்கப்பட்டும் உள்ள நூல்களே சிறந்த கருவியாகும். இவற்றுள்ளும் புறநானூறு சிறந்தது. அந்நூலின் முதற் செய்யுள் சேரமான் பெருஞ்சோற்றுதியன் சேரலாதன் என்பானை முரஞ்சியூர் முடிநாகர் பாடியது. இச் சேரலாதன் பாரத யுத்தத்திற் பாண்டவர் பக்கல் நின்று அப்பெரும்போர் முடியுந்துணையும் பாண்டவ சேனைக்கு உணவளிக்கும் அருஞ்செயலை மேற்கொண்டு புரிந்தவன். இக் காரணம் பற்றியே "பெருஞ்சோற்றுதியன்" என்னும் அடையுடன் வழங்கப்பட்டான். அவன் அத்தொழில் புரிந்த செய்தி,

> "அலங்குளைப் புரவி யைவரொடு சினைஇ
> நிலந்தலைக் கொண்ட பொலம்பூந் தும்பை
> ஈரைம் பதின்மரும் பொருதுகளத் தொழியப்
> பெருஞ்சோற்று மிகுபதம் வரையாது கொடுத்தோய்

என அப்புறநானூற்றுப் பாடலிலேயே அவ்வரசனை முடிநாகர் முன்னிலைப் படுத்துக் கூறுதலால் உணர்க. இதனால் அச்செய்யுள் பாடிய முடிநாகரும் அப்பாடல் பெற்ற பெருஞ்சோற்றுதியனும் ஒரேகாலத்தவ ரென்பதும் இப்பாடல் பாரத யுத்தம் முடிந்த சமீபகாலத்தே பாடப்பட்ட தென்பதும் இனிது விளங்கும். இவ்வுதியன் பாண்டவ சேனைக்கு பெருஞ்சோறு கொடுத்து உதவிய வரலாற்றைப் பண்டைக் காலத்துப் புலவர் சிலரும் புகழ்ந்து பாடியிருக்கின்றனர். இவனை அகநானூற்றில்,

"மறப்படைக் குதிரை மாறு மைந்தற்
றறக்க மெய்திய தொய்யா நல்லிசை
முதியர்ப் பேணிய உதியஞ் சேரல்
பெருஞ்சோறு கொடுத்த ஞான்றை யிரும்பல்
கூளிச் சுற்றங் குடியிருந் தாங்கு."

என மாமூலனாரும்,

"ஓரைவ ரீரைம் பதின்ம ருடன்றெழுந்த
போரிற் பெருஞ்சோறு போற்றாது தானளித்த,
சேரன்"

என சிலப்பதிகாரத்தில் இளங்கோவடிகளும் பாடியிருத்தல் காண்க. இவற்றுள், முன்னதிற் பெருஞ்சோறு கொடுத்தவன் உதியன் என்னும் பெயருடையவனே என்று விளக்கப் பட்டுள்ளது. இனி இவ்வுதியனை முன்னிலையில் வைத்துப் பாடிய முடிநாகரும் தலைச்சங்கப் புலவர் வரிசையில் நூல்களிற் கூறப்படும் முடிநாகரும் ஒருவரே என்பதைக் காட்டற்கு, அவ்விரண்டிடங்களிலும் "முரஞ்சியூர்" என ஊர் ஒன்று யிருத்தலே தக்க சான்றாகும். அன்றியும் இம்முடிநாகர் தமிழ் நூற்களிற் காணும் புலவ ரெல்லாரினும் மிகப்பழமை யுடையராகத் தெரிதலால், அப்பழமை யொன்றே அவரைப் பாரதகாலத்தவ ரென்று உறுதி கூறத் தக்கது.

மேற்குறித்த புலவரது பெயரை நோக்கின், பாரதகாலத்தில் பரதகண்ட மெங்கும் பரவிப் பெருவலி பெற்ற "நாகர்" என்ற சாதியினராகத் தோற்றுகின்றார். அவ்யுத்த காலத்தில் நாகர்கள் பரதகண்ட மெங்கும் பரவி யிருந்தமையும், அதன் பிற்காலத்தே அருச்சுனன் வழித்தோன்றலாகிய ஜனமேஜயன் இவர் குலத்தை வேரறுத்தமையும், மகாபாரதத்தின் சரித நுட்பங்களாகும். இவர்கள் தங்கள் முடிமேல் ஐந்தலை முத்தலைகளை யுடைய நாக வடிவமுடைய தொன்றைத் தரித்து வந்தமையால், அது பற்றி, இவர்கட்கு நாகர் என்ற பெயர் வழங்குவ தாயிற்று. இவ்வாறு முடியில் நாக வடிவினைத் தரித்துவந்த அந்நாகரது கற்சிலைகள், பழங்காலத்தனவாக, இன்றும் வடஇந்தியாவிற் பல

விடங்களில் உள்ளன. இனி, நாம் கூறிவந்த தலைச்சங்கப் புலவரும் அக்கூட்டத்தில் ஒருவரென்பதற்கு "முடிநாகர்" என இவர்க்கு வழங்கும் பெயரே தக்க சான்றாம். இம்முடிநாகரது வாக்காகப் புறநானூற்றிற் கண்ட பாடலால், நிலம், நீர், தீ, வளி, ஆகாயம் என்னும் பஞ்சபூதங்களை வணங்கும் பழைய வழக்கம் இவர் காலத் திருந்த தென்பதும், நான்கு வேதப் பகுப்பு இவர் காலத்தே அமைந்திருந்த தென்பதும், இமயமலைச் சாரலில் அந்தணர் பலர் வசித்தனர் என்பதும் பிறவும் அறியலாகும்.

ஆசிரியர் நச்சினார்க்கினியர் "அறுவகைப்பட்டப் பார்ப்பன பக்கமும்" என்னுந் தொல்காப்பியச் சூத்திர வுரையில் தலைச் சங்ககாலத்திருந்தவராக வான்மீகனார், மார்க்கண்டேயனார், கௌதமனார் இவர்களைக் கூறுகின்றார். ஆயின், இவர்களும் பாரத காலத்தை யொட்டி யிருந்தவ ராதல் வேண்டும். இவருள் வான்மீகனார் இயற்றிய பாடலொன்று புறநானூற்று கூகூ-ஆம் செய்யுளாக வுள்ளது. இப்பாடல் தவத்தின் பெருமையை மட்டும் விளக்கி நிற்பது. அது வருமாறு:—

"பருதி சூழ்ந்தஇப் பயங்கெழு மாநிலம்
ஒருபக லெழுவ ரெய்தி யற்றே;
வையமுந் தவமுந் தூக்கிற் றவத்துக்'
ஐயவி யனைத்தும் ஆற்றா தாகலிற்
கைவிட் டனரே காதலர்; அதனால்
விட்டோரை விடாஅள் திருவே,
விடாஅ தோர் இவள் விடப்பட் டோரே."

என்பதாம். இவ்வாறே மார்க்கண்டேயனார் பாடலொன்றும் அத்தொகை நூலில் கூகூ-ஆம் செய்யுளாகக் காணப்படுகின்றது. அது வருமாறு:—

"மயக்கிருள் கருவிய விசும்பு முகனாக
இயங்கிய விருசுடர் கண்ணெனப் பெயரிய
வளியிடை வழங்கா வழக்கரு நீத்தம்
வயிரக் குறட்டின் வயங்குமணி யாத்துப்
பொன்னந் திகிரி முன்சமத் துருட்டிப்
முன்னோர் செல்லவும் செல்லா தின்னும்

விலைலப் பெண்டிரிற் பலர்மீக் கூற
வுள்ளேன் வாழியர் யானெனப் பன்மா
ணிலமக ளழுத காஞ்சியு
முண்டென வுரைப்பரா லுணர்ந்திசி னோரே."

தலைச்சங்க காலத்தவ ராகிய இம் மார்க்கண்டேயனாரால ஒரு காஞ்சி நூல் இயற்பட்டுள்ள தென்றுந் தெரிகிறது. இவர்கள் நூலைத் "தலையாய ஓத்து" என்பார் நச்சினார்க்கினியார்.

இனி, அடுத்தவராகிய கோதமனாரைக் குறித்துச் சில விஷயங்கள் அதிகமாகக் கூறலாம். புறநானூற்றில் கோதமனாரென்னும் புலவர் தரும புத்திரனைப் பாடிய பாடலொன்று ௩௬௬-ஆம் செய்யுளாக வுள்ளது. இப்பாடல் இடையிடையே சிதைந்து காணப்படுகின்றது. அப்புலவர் இப்பாடலில் தரும புத்திரனை "அறவோன் மகனே" என விளிக்கின்றார். இங்குக் காட்டிய தருமபுத்திரன் பாண்டவர் முன்றோன்றலே யாயின், கௌதமனார் பாரதகாலத்தவர் ஆவர்; ஆயின், தலைச்சங்க காலமும் அதுவே யெனக் கூறுதல் தானே அமையும். பாரத காலத்திலும் அதன் முற்காலத்திலும் தமிழ்மொழி பரதகண்ட மெங்கும் பரவியிருந்த தென்பதற்குச் சில பல குறிப்புகள் காணப்படுகின்றன. ஆரியாவர்த்தத்தே தமிழின் பாகதமாகிய பாஷைகள் இன்றும் வழங்குகின்றன என்னும் பிரசித்தக் கொள்கையே இதனை வலியுறுத்தும். ஆயின், கௌதமனார் "அறவோன் மகனை" (தருமபுத்திரனை) யடைந்து தமிழ்ப்பாவால் அவனைப் பாடி மகிழ்வித்திருத்தலிலும் வியப்பொன்றில்லை.

இனிப் "பதிற்றுப்பத்து" ஆசிரியரில் பாலைக்கௌதமனார் என்னும் புலவ ரொருவர் உளர். அந் நூன் மூன்றாம் பத்து அவர் பாடியதாகும். தலைச்சங்கத்தவராக நச்சினார்க்கினியர் குறித்த கௌதமனாரே இப்பதிற்றுப்பத்துக் கௌதமனார் என்று கருதற்குச் சில ஆதாரங்கள் உள்ளன. பதிற்றுப்பத்தில் பாலைக்கௌதமனாராற் புகழப்பட்டவன் பல்யானைச் செல்கெழு குட்டுவன் என்னுஞ் சேர னாவன். இவன் இமயவரம்பன் நெடுஞ்சேரலாதன் தம்பி எனவும், இவ்விருவரும் உதியஞ்சேரல் என்பானுடைய மக்கள்

ளெனவும் பதிற்றுப்பத்தின் 2, 3-ஆம் பத்துக்களின் பதிகங்க ளால் விளங்குவன வாம். "உதியஞ்சேரல்" என்னும் பெயர் பாரதப் போரில் பாண்டவ சேனைக்கு உணவளித்த சோழனுக்கு வழங்குகின்றமை முன்னமே அறிவிக்கப்பட்டது. ஆகவே, அவன் மக்களாகிய இமயவரம்பன் நெடுஞ்சேரலாதனும் பல் யானைச் செல்கெழு குட்டுவனும் பாரத காலத்தை அடுத் திருந்தவ ரென்பதுந் தானே பெறப்படும். இவருள் இளையவனாகிய குட்டு வனைப் பாடிய பாலைக் கௌதமனாரே தருமபுத்திரனைப் பாடிய கௌதமனா ரென்பதற்கு இருவர் காலமும் ஒன்றுதல் சான்றாம். பாலைக் கௌதமனார் என்னும் அடை புணர்க்கப்பட்டதன் கார ணம், குட்டுவனை அவர் பாடிய மூன்றாம்பத்து முழுதும் பாலைத் திணை பற்றி வந்தமையே யன்றி வேறில்லை. உதியஞ்சேரல் மக்களிருவரும் செய்த செயல்கள், பிந்திய கடைச் சங்கம் புல்வ ரால், சேரர்களது ஆதிமுன்னோர் புரிந்த செய்கைகளாகப் புக ழப்படுகின்றன. அன்றியும் பாலைக் கௌதமனார் பல்யானைச்செல் கெழு குட்டுவனைப் பாடிச் சுவர்க்கம் பெற்றார் என வழங்கும் கதையும், கடைச்சங்க காளிற் பழஞ் செய்தியாக வழங்கப்பட்டு வந்ததென்பது "நான் மறையாளன் செய்யுட் கொண்டு மேனிலை யுலகம் விடுத்தோனாயினும்" எனச் சிலப்பதிகாரத்து வருதலால் விளங்கும்.

உதியஞ் சேரலது மூத்த மகனாகிய இமயவரம்பன் நெடுஞ் சேரலாதனைக் குமட்டூர்க் கண்ணனார் பாடிய இரண்டாம் பத்தில், "கவிர்ததை சிலம்பிற் றுஞ்சுங் கவரி, பரந்திலங் கருவிய நரந்தங் கனவும், ஆரியர் துவன்றிய பேரிசை யிமயம்" என வருதலால் அக்காலத்தில், ஆரியரது பிரவேசம் இமயமலைச் சாரலில் அதிக மா யிருந்த தென்பது விளங்கும். இவ்வாறே "அந்தி யந்தணர் அருங்கட னிறுக்கும் பொற்கோட் டிமயம்" என்றார் முரஞ்சியூர் முடிநாகரும். கொடைக்குப் பெயர்போன வள்ளலாக அப்புலவர் காலத்து விளங்கியவன் கௌரவர்க்குத் துணையாயிருந்த யாதவ னாகிய அக்குரூரன் என்பான். இவனைத் தலையேழு வள்ளல்களில்

ஒருவனென்று சொல்லுவர். தலைச்சங்க நாளில் இவன் பிரசித்தி பெற்றிருந்தவனென்பது, "போர்தலை மிகுத்த ஈரைம் பதின்மரொடு, துப்புத் துறைபோகிய துணிவுடையாண்மை, அக்குரன் அனைய கைவண்மையையே" எனக் குமட்டூர்க் கண்ணனார் பாடுதலால் விளங்கும். பாலைக் கௌதமனார் பாடிய மூன்றாம் பத்தில், உதியஞ்சேரலது இளைய மகனாகிய பல்யானைச் செல்கெழு குட்டுவனது செய்கைகளுள் "மதியுறழ் மரபின் முதியரைத் தழீஇ" என்பதும் ஒன்றாகப் பதிகத்துட் கூறப்படுகின்றது. பதிற்றுப்பத்து உரைகாரர் இவ்வடிக்கு உரிய பொருள் கூறினராகத் தோற்றவில்லை. இவ் அடியில் வந்த "முதியர்" என்னும் சொல் பாண்டவரைக் குறிப்பதாகும். பல்யானைச் செல்கெழுகுட்டுவன் காலத்திற் பஞ்சவர் வயோதிகம் பெற்று விளங்கினமையால் அப்பெயர் பெற்றனராவர். பாண்டவர்க்கு "முதியர்" என்னும் சொல்வழக்கம் தொன்றுதொட்டு உண்டென்பது, மேலே நாம் மாமூலனார் வாக்காக அகநானூற்றினின்றுங் காட்டிய "மறப்படைக் குதிரை மாறா மைந்திற்- றுறக்க மெய்திய தொய்யா நல்லிசை- முதியர்ப் பேணிய வுதியஞ்சேரல்" என்புழியும் பயின்றிருத்தல் காண்க. அம் முதியரென்னும் பெயர் பாண்டவரையே குறிப்பதென்பதை அதற்கு விசேடணமாக "மதியுறழ் மரபின்" என்னும் பதங்கள் புணர்க்கப்பட்டிருத்தலே நன்கு விளக்கும். இவ்விசேடண பதங்களின் பொருள் "சந்திரனோடு பொருந்தி வரும் வமிசத்தவராகிய" முதியர் என்பதாம். தந்தையாகிய உதியஞ்சேரல் பாண்டவரைப் பேணியது போல, அவனிளைய மகனாகிய குட்டுவனும் போற்றினமையால், அவன் செய்கைகளுள் 'மதியுறழ் மரபின் முதியரைத் தழுவியதும்' ஒன்றாக எடுத்துப் புகழப்பட்டதென்க. இவற்றால், உதியஞ்சேரல் மக்களாகிய இமயவரம்பன் நெடுஞ்சேரலாதனும் பல்யானைச் செல்கெழு குட்டுவனும், இவ்விருவரையும் முறையே பாடிய குமட்டூர்க்கண்ணனாரும், பாலைக் கௌதமனாரும் பாரத யுத்தம் நிகழ்ந்த காலத்தை ஒட்டி வசித்தவரென்பது வெள்ளிடைமலைபோல் விளங்கும்.

மேற்காட்டிய சேரரிருவரும் உதியஞ்சேரற்கு, வெளியன் என்னும் வேளின் மகளாகிய நல்லினி வயிற்றிற் பிறந்தவர் என்பதும் அவருள் மூத்தவன் இமயத்தில் விற்பொறித்துத் தமிழகம் முழுதும் தன்கோல் நிறுவியும், இமயச்சாரலில் வசித்த ஆரியரை வென்றும், மிலேச்ச அரசரைப் பிணித்துச் சிறையிட்டும் இவ்வாறு ஐம்பத்தெட்டியாண்டு ஆட்சி புரிந்தவனென்பதும், இளையவனாகிய குட்டுவன் உம்பற்காடு, அகப்பா என்ற இடங்களில் வென்றும், பெரியோராகிய பஞ்சவரை வழிபட்டும், பெரியபூமிகளைப் பலர்க்குப் பகுத்தளித்தும், நெடும்பாரதாயனார் என்னும் புரோகிதரைப் பெற்றும் இவ்வாறு பல சிறப்புகளுடன் இருபத்தைந்து வருஷம் ஆட்சி புரிந்தவனென்பதும் பதிற்றுப்பத்துப் பதிகங்களால் விளங்குகின்றன. குமட்டூர்க் கண்ணனாரும் பாலைக் கௌதமனாரும் பாடிய பத்துக்களால் அதிகமாகச் சரித்திர விசேடங்கள் அறிதற்கில்லையாயினும், அவற்றிற் கண்ட பாடல்கள் தமிழ் மொழியின் தொன்மை மாட்சியையும் சிறப்பையும் நன்றாய் விளக்கற்குரியன. அவை ஒவ்வொன்றையும் எடுத்து விரிப்பதற்கு இடம் இதுவன்றாகலின் விடப்பட்டன.

இனிப் பாரத யுத்தகாலம் இற்றைக்கு 5,000 ஆண்டுகட்கு முன்பு என்பது நமக்குள் வழங்கும் மரபாகும். ஆனால் சுதேச மேதாவிகள் சிலரும் விதேச அறிஞர் பலரும் ஆராய்ச்சி முறையிற் பல்லாற்றானும் சோதித்து வருவதில், முற்காட்டிய காலத்தினின்றும் பெரிதும் வேறுபட்டு பற்பலவாறு அபிப்பிராய முறுகின்றனர். இவ் வபிப்பிராய பேதங்களில் உள்ள தாரதம்மியங்களையெல்லாம் நன்கு பரிசோதித்து அவற்றிலொன்றும் பொருந்திய தாகாமை காட்டிச் சித்தூர் வி. கோபாலையரவர்கள் பிரபலமான பதினொரு தக்க காரணங்களால், கி.மு. 12-ம் நூற்றாண்டின் ஆரம்பமே பாரதயுத்த காலமென்று, படிப்போர் மகிழ்ந்து உவக்கும்படி, தாம் வெளியிட்ட ஆங்கில (Chronology of Ancient India) நூலில் காட்டியிருக்கின்றனர். இவரது கொள்கையைச் சரிதவாராய்ச்சி வல்லார் பலர் உண்மையுடையதென்று துணிந்திருக்கின்றார். இவ்வாறு அக்கொள்கை என்றும்

அசைவு பெறாது வலிபெறுமாயின், நமக்கு முப்பத்தொரு நூற்றாண்டுகட்கு முந்திய பாரதயுத்த காலத்தையொட்டி, முரஞ்சியூர் முடிநாகராயர், கௌதமனார், வான்மீகையர், மார்க்கண்டேயனார், குமட்டூர்க்கண்ணனார் முதலிய புலவர்கள் தலைச்சங்கத் திருந்து தமிழ் வளர்த்தார்க ளென்று முடிக்கலாம். *

அகஸ்தியர் தமிழ்நாட்டுக்காடுகளைத் திருத்தி, ஆண்டுக் கண்ணபிரான் வழியினராய வேளிர் பலரைக் குடியேற்றிவைத்தா ரென்ற செய்தி நச்சினார்க்கினியர்து எழுத்துக்களால் விளங்குகின்றது. இச்சரித்திரம் உண்மையுடையதாயின், அகஸ்தியர் பாரதகாலத்தை யொட்டியே தென்னாட்டுக்கு வந்தன்ரென்று கொள்ளல் நேரும். கபிலரென்னும் புலவர்பெருமான் இருங்கோவேள் என்பானைப் புகழுமிடத்து "நாற்பத்தொன்பது வழிமுறைவந்த வேளிருள் வேளே" எனக் கூறுதலால், ஏறக்குறைய நமக்கு மூவாயிரம் ஆண்டுகட்கு முன்னர் வேளிரின் ஆதிமுதல்வர் அகஸ்தியரால் தென்னாட்டுக்கழைக்கப்பட்டனர் என்று தெளியலாம். இதனை விரிவாக "வேழிர் வரலாறு" என்பதிற் காட்டியுள்ளோம். இவற்றால், தலைச்சங்கமிருந்த அகஸ்தியனாரும், அம்மகாபாரதகாலத்து விளங்கினவரென்று பெறப்படுகின்றது. *

இதுகாறும் கூறிவந்த செய்திகளால், மகாபாரதகாலத்தில் தமிழ்மொழி பரதகண்ட மெங்கும் பாவிச்சிறந்த புலவர் பலரைப்பெற்று விளங்கிய தென்பது ஒருவாறு விளங்கும்.

* [தலைச்சங்கம் இருந்தாருள், அகத்தியனாரும் நிதிக்கிழவனார் வான்மீகையாரும் மார்க்கண்டேயரும் முடிநாகரும் கௌதமரும் காணப்படுகின்றார். ஆயினும் அவர் யாவரும் ஒரே காலத்தின ரல்லர். அச்சங்கம் 89 பாண்டியர் ஆதரவில் ஏறக்குறைய 1500 வருடங்கள் நிலைபெற்றதாகும். ஆகவே, அகத்தியனாரும் நிதிக்கிழவனும் இராமாயண காலத்தை யடுத்துச் சங்கத்தின் முதற்பகுதியிலும், வான்மீகையாரும் மார்க்கண்டேயரும் அதன் இடைப்பகுதியிலும், கௌதமரும் முடிநாகரும் பாரத காலத்தை யடுத்துச் சங்கத்துக் கடைப்பகுதியிலும் இருந்தோர் ஆவர். நச்சினார்க்கினியார் "விலங்கடந்த நெடுமுடியண்ணல்" என்றது கண்ணபிரானை யன்று என்பர் ஸ்ரீமான். கார்த்திகேய முதலியார். அவர் கூற்றில் பெரிதும் உண்மையுளது. "முச்சங்கமும் இறையனார் பொருளுரையும்" என்ற வியாசத்தின் கீழ் இவ்விஷயம் எழுத்தாளப்படும். பத்திராதிபர்.]

LANKA AND THE TAMIL SANGAMS.

ஈழநாடும் தமிழ்ச்சங்கமும்.*

BY

MR. A. MUTUTTHAMBY PILLAI AVL., *(Jaffna.)*

முதற்சங்க முதலாய முச்சங்கத்திலும் விளங்கிய புலவர் பல்லாயிரவர். அவர்கள் ஒரு ஜாதியினரும் ஒரு சமயத்தினரும் ஒரு தேயத்தினரும் ஒரு தொழிலினரும் அல்லர். அவர்கள் பல ஜாதியாளரும் பல சமயிகளும் பல தேயத்தினரும் வேறுபட்ட தொழிலினரு மாயே யிருந்தா ரென்பது அவர்கள் பெயரூர் முதலியவற்றால் நன்கு துணியப்படும்.

தமிழ்நாடு, செந்தமிழ்நாடும் கொடுந்தமிழ்நாடுமென, இரு பாற்படும். அவற்றை மருவிச் சூழ்ந்துள்ள நாடுகள் பதினேழு. அவை, "சிங்களஞ் சோனகஞ் சாவகஞ் சீனந் துளுக் குடகம், கொங்கணங் கன்னடங் கொல்லந் தெலுங்கங் கலிங்கம் வங்கம், கங்க மகதங் கவுடங் கடாரங் கடுங்குசலம், தங்கும் புகழ்த்தமிழ் சூழ்பதி னேழ்புவி தாமிவையே" என்பதால் பெறப்படும்.

அவற்றுள், சிங்களம் என்பது தென்பாண்டி புன்னாடுகளுக் கணித்தா யுள்ளது. ஈழம் என்பது சிங்களத்தின் பரியாயமும் பகுதியு மா யடங்கு மென்பது இலக்கண விளக்கம்—"செந்தமிழ் நிலஞ்சேர்" என்னுஞ் சூத்திரவுரையாற் கொள்ளப்படும். மண்டலப்பெயர் கொண்டு விளங்கும் நாடுகளுள்ளே ஈழமு மொன்றாம். சேரமண்டலம் சோழமண்டலம் பாண்டிமண்டலம் ஈழமண்டலம் தொண்டைமண்டலம் எனவருதல் காண்க.

* Reprinted from the "Sen-Tamil" with kind permission.

சிங்கள மென்னும் பெயர் சிங்குவாகுவின் புத்திரன் ஆண்டமையால் வந்த தென்பது பொருந்தாது. சிங்குவாகுவின் புத்திரன் இலங்கைக்கு வந்தது இன்றைக்கு இரண்டாயிரத்தைஞ்நூறு வருஷங்களுக்கு முன்னராம். இற்றைக்கு மூவாயிரம் வருஷங்களுக்கு முன்னுள்ள பாரதத்திலே சிங்கள மென்னும் பெயர் கேட்கப்படுகின்றது. இலங்கைக்குச் சிங்களமென்னும் பெயர் அங்குள்ள கறுவாப்பட்டையால் வந்தது. சிங்களம் என்பதன்பொருள் பட்டை. சிங்களத்துவீபம்-பட்டைத்தீவு.

சிங்களத்தீவின் வடபாகமும் கீழ்பாகமுமே பெரும்பாலும் ஈழமண்டல மென வழங்கப்பட்டது. இவ்வீழ மண்டலம் இலங்கைக்கு விஜயராஜன் வந்த (543 B. C.) காலத்துக்குமுன், அஃதாவது இரண்டாயிரத்து நானூறு வருஷத்துக்கு முன்னர் தமிழ்மக்கள் குடிகொண்டிருந்த நாடாம். இவ்வுண்மை விஜயராஜன் வரும்போது திருக்கேதீச்சரம் சிலமா யிருந்த தென்றும், பின்னாதனை அவன் சீரணோத்தாரணம் பண்ணுவித்தா னென்றும் வரும் 'வைபவமாலை' யாற் றுணியப்படும் (*vide* Brito's Vaibava malai.)

இன்னும் பாலாவி, மாதோட்டம், மாந்தை என்னும் தமிழ்ச் சொற்கள் இடப்பெயராய்ப் பண்டைக் காலந் தொட்டு அங்கே வழங்குதலும், தேவாரத்திலே பாலாவி, மாதோட்டம், திருக்கேதீச்சரம் திரிகோணமலை என்னும் பெயர்கள் வருதலும், பேட்டோலக்சி, பென்னட் (Bertolocci, Bennet) முதலிய ஐரோப்பிய பண்டிதர்கள் எழுதிய இலங்கை வரலாற்றில் "விஜயன் வருதற்குப் பன்னெடுங்காலத்துக்கு முன்னே தமிழர் இலங்கையிற் குடிகொண்டிருந்தார்கள்" எனக் கூறுதலும், ராயல் ஏஷியாடிக் சொசைட்டியாரது பத்திரிகையிலே, (Journal of the Royal Asiatic Society, Ceylon Branch, 1148, p. 73.) "ரோமர் இலங்கையிலே வர்த்தகஞ்செய்த காலத்திலே தமிழர் மாதோட்டத்தை இராசதானியாகக் கொண்டு அரசு செய்தார்கள்" என்றும், "அவ்வரசு விசயன்காலத்துக்கும் யாழ்ப்பாடி காலத்துக்கும் மிகவும் முந்திய பழமையினை யுடையது" என்றும் வருவன இதற்குப் பிரமாணமாம்.

இவ்வாறு இலங்கையில் அரசுகொண்டிருந்த தமிழரசர் சோழ பாண்டி மண்டலத் திராச பரம்பரையினரும் அவரோடு கலப்புடையருமா யிருந்தார்கள். அவர்கள் மாதோட்டத்திலே கட்டியிருந்த கோட்டை மிக்க வலிமையும் அழகும் அற்புதமு முடையது. பெரு மரக்கலங்கள் மன்னார்க்கடலில் வருமாயின் அவைகளைத் தன்மாட் டிழுத்துக்கொள்ளும் காந்தப்பொறி யுடையதா யிருந்த தென்பர். இத்துணைச் சிறந்த நாகரிகம் வாய்ந்த அந் நகரத்து மக்கள் தமிழ்க் கல்வியிலே பேரபிமானமும் பாண்டித்தியமு முடையராயே விளங்கின ராதல் வேண்டும். அவர்கள் காலம் முதற்சங்கமும் இடைச்சங்கமும் நடைபெற்ற காலம். அச் சங்கங்கள் நடைபெற்ற நகரங்களுமோ மிகச்சமீபத்தே எதிர்க் கரையிலே யிருந்தன.

மாதோட்டத்துப் புலவர்க்கு அக்கரையிலே யுள்ள சங்கமும், அக்கரையிலே யுள்ள புலவர்க்கு இக்கரையிலேயுள்ள இராச சபையும், பிரபுக்கள் மிகுதியும், திருக்கேத்தீச்சர சிவாலயமும் காதற் பொருளா மன்றோ? அதனால் அங்குள்ளார் இங்கும், இங்குள்ளார் அங்கும் போக்குவர வுடையராயிருந்தனர். தமிழ்ச்சங்கத்திலே ஆசனம் பெற்று வீற்றிருத்தற்குச் சிங்காசனம் பெற்ற அரசரும் விரும்பித் தம்புலமை காட்டினரென்றால் அக்காலத்தில் அச்சங்கப் பலகை யேற்றம் போலும் பெரும்பேறும் பெரும் போகமும் வேறில்லை யெனல் வேண்டும். எனவே ஈழநாட்டுப் புலவரும் அரசரும் அதனைப் பெரிதும் விரும்பின ராதல் வேண்டும்.

> "யாதானு நாடாமா லூராமால் என்னொருவன்
> சாந்துணையுங் கல்லாத வாறு"

இத்திருவாக்குக் கொடுந்தமிழ் நாட்டிலே புலைக்குலத்திலே பிறந்தவரும் கடைச்சங்கப்பலகையேறித் தம்மைப்பிரமதேவரது அமிசாவதாரமென நாட்டினவருமாகிய தெய்வப்புலமைத் திருவள்ளுவ நாயனாரது சுவானுபவ மன்றோ? இவ்வுண்மை முந்திய சங்கத்தாருக்கு மொப்பா மன்றோ? அதனை ஈழநாட்டு மக்கள் கடைப்பிடியா திருந்தவர் அல்லர். ஆகவே ஈழநாட்டுப் புலவர்களும் அரசரும் தமிழ்ச்சங்க மேறி யிருந்தா ராதல் வேண்டும்.

முதற்சங்கத்திலே யிருந்த முடிநாகர் என்பவர் ஈழநாட்டு வேந்த ராதல் வேண்டும். இலங்கையிலே விஜயராஜன் காலத்துக்கு முன்னே நெடுங்காலம் அரசுசெய்தவர்கள் நாகராயரென்னும் பெயர் புனைந்திருந்தனர். முன்னொரு காலத்திலே இலங்கையிலே நாகர்கள் மிக்க நாகரீகமும் பராக்கிரமமு முடையராயிருந்தாரென்பதும், அவர்கள் இராச்சியம் ஒரு காலத்திலே இமயம் வரைக்கும் வியாபித்திருந்ததென்பதும், நாகபட்டினம், நாகபுரம் முதலிய நகரப் பெயர்களால் அநுமிக்கப்படும். நாக கன்னிகை வயிற்றிலே சோழராஜனுக்குப் புத்திரனாய்ப் பிறந்து நாகபட்டினம் போய்த் தந்தையைக் கண்டு தொண்டை நாட்டுக்கு அரசனாய்ப் முடிசூட்டப் பெற்றவன் ஒருவ னுளன் என்பது பத்துப்பாட்டிலே கூறப்படுகின்றது. அந்நாக கன்னிகை இந்நாகர் குலக்கொடி யாதல் வேண்டும். இந்நாகர்கள் பிற் காலத்திலே தமிழரால் அடிப்படுத்தப்பட் டரசிழந்து சுருங்கினார்கள். அவர் வழிவந்தோரே இக்காலத்திலே விந்தனையி லுள்ள வேடரென்பது அநேகர் துணிபு. (See *Sketches of Ceylon History*, by P. Arunachalam, M.A., Cantab.)

இன்னும் ஈழநாட்டிலே நாகர்கோயில் என்னும் பெயரால் ஓரூர் உளது. யாழ்ப்பாணம் பூர்வம் சிங்களரால் நாகத்தீவு என வழங்கப்பட்டது. இதுவும் பூர்வம் நாகர்கள் இங்கிருந்தமைக்குச் சான்றாம். அரசிழந்த நாகர்கள் ஒருகாலத்தில் யாழ்ப்பாணத்திலும் விந்தனைப் பகுதியிலும் நயினார்தீவிலும் போய் ஒதுங்கியிருந்தனராதல் வேண்டும்.

இன்னும் கடைச்சங்கத்தி லிருந்த இளநாகனாரும் இலங்கை அரசரு ளொருவராதல் வேண்டும். இளநாகன் என்னும் பெயருடைய அரசர் ஒருவர் கிறிஸ்தாப்தம் 38-ல் அரசு செய்தவர். அவர் பின்னர் அரசிழந்து பாண்டிநாடு சென்று அங்கே சிறிது காலம் வசித்துப் பாண்டியன் கொடுத்த சேனைகொண்டு தமதாசு மீட்டவர். அவர் அங்கிருந்த காலத்தில் இறையனாரகப் பொருளுரை கேட்டார் போலும். இறையனாரகப் பொருளுரையை ஆசிரிய பரம்பரையாகப் பாடங் கேட்டாருள்ளே இளநாகரும்

ஒருவராகக் கூறப்படுவர். அவர் முசிறி யாசிரியர் நீலகண்டனார்க் குரைத்தாரெனக் கூறப்படுதலால் நீலகண்டனார் அவர்க்கு மாணாக்கர் ஆவார். முசிறி என ஈழ நாட்டகத்து மோரூர் உளது. ஆதலின் நீலகண்டனாரும் ஈழநாட்டுப் புலவராதல் வேண்டும்.

இன்னும் மாந்தையிலும் மணற்றியிலும் பாண்டியர் போர் புரிந்து பெற்ற கொற்றமும் இறையனாரகப் பொருட்கோவையிற் கூறப்படுகின்றது. மாந்தையென்பது மாதோட்டத்துக்குச் சமீபத்தேயுள்ள ஊர். மணற்றியென்பது யாழ்ப்பாணம். இது மணல் நாடு என்றும் மணற்றிடல் என்றும் ஒருகாலம் வழங்கப்பட்டது. இலங்கையரசர் பாண்டியரோடும் சோழர்களோடும் எதிர்பொருதற்கு இஃதொரு காலம் போர்க்கள மாகவு மிருந்தது. இதன் பகுதிகளுளொன்று இன்றும் களபூமி யென்னும் பெயரால் வழங்கும். மாந்தையிலும் மணற்றியிலும் கிறிஸ்தாப்தத்துக்கு முன்னே 103-ம் வருஷத்தில் ஒரு பெரிய யுத்தம் நடந்தது. அதிலே பாண்டியர் வாலகம்பாகுவைப் புறங்கண்டு அவன் மனைவியையும் புத்த பாத்திரத்தையும் கவர்ந்துகொண் டேகியதோடு ஈழநாட்டையும் தமதடிப்படுத்திப் போயினர் என மகாவமிசங் கூறுகின்றது.

இன்னும் சிலப்பதிகாரத்துக் குரை செய்த அடியார்க்கு நல்லாரும் ஈழநாட்டா ரெனப்படுவார். அவர் குணபூஷண சிங்காரிய ராஜாவுக்கு மந்திரியா யிருந்து ஈழநாட்டில் அநேக தருமாலயங் களும் வித்தியாசாலைகளும் ஸ்தாபித்தவர். அவர் அமைப்பித்த திருக்குளம் இன்று முளது. அஃது "அடியார்க்கு நல்லார் குளம்" என வழங்குகின்றது. அது வண்ணைச் சிவாலயத்துச் சந்நிதித் தெருவி லுள்ளது. அதற் கயலிலே அவர் தமது அரசன் பெயராலே அமைப்பித்த குளம் "ஆரியகுளம்" என இக்காலத்து வழங்குகின்றது. அவர் இருந்த மனையிலமும் அவர் பெயராலே வழங்குகின்றது. அவர் காலத்திலே தமிழ் யாழ்ப்பாணத்திலே மிக விருத்தி பெற்றது. அவரே அறுபத்துமூன்று நாயன்மாருக் கும் ஆலயமும் பூசைக்கு நிபந்தமும் யாழ்ப்பாணத்தில் முதன் முதல் வகுத்தவர். அவ்வாலயமிருந்த இடம் "நாயன்மார்கட்டு" என இன்றும் வழங்குகின்றது.

முதிரம், மாங்கை என்னும் பெயர்களையும் தம்பிக்கு அஞ்சிக் காடு கொண்டிருந்த ஸ்ரீசங்கபோதியினது சரித்திரத்தையும் நோக்கும் போது.

"அந்நாள் வந்திலை யருங்கவிப் புலவோய்
இந்நாள் வந்துநீ நொந்தெனை யடைந்தாய்
தலைதனைக் கொடுபோய்த் தம்பிகைக் கொடுத்ததன்
விலைதனை மீட்டுன் வெறுமைநோய் களையே".
"வெம்புங் காலை வெதம்பி விழுஞ்சிரம்
செம்பொன் கோடி விலையெனச் சிந்தித்தான்
உம்பர் நாடு முலகினுந் தேடினும்
எம்பி போலெமக் கியாவ ரினியரே."

எனக்கூறிய குமணனும் ஈழநாட்டிலுள்ளான் எனத்துணிதற் கிடமாகின்றது. ஸ்ரீசங்கபோதியினது இயற்பெயர் குமணன் போலும். மகாவமிசத்திலே கூறப்படும் ஸ்ரீ சங்கபோதி சரித்திரமும் புறநானூற்றிலும் பிறவற்றிலும் வருங் குமணன் சரித்திரமும் அவர் காலமும் பெரிது மொத்திருக்கின்றன.

யாழ்ப்பாணத்திலே யுள்ள செம்பியன்பற்று, பல்லவராயன் கட்டு, தொண்டைமானாறு, பாண்டியன்றாழ்வு முதலிய இடப்பெயர்களை நோக்குமிடத்துத் தமிழ்நாட்டு வேந்தர்கள் யாழ்ப்பாணத் தொடர்புடையரா யிருந்தாரென்பது நன்கு துனியப்படும்.

இன்னும் மாதோட்டத்துக்குத் தெற்கே யுள்ள குதிரைமலை மிக்க பழைமையும் யவனதேசம் வரையும் பரந்த கீர்த்தியு முடையது. அஃதொரு காலம் சிற்றரசர்க்கு இருக்கையாயு மிருந்தது. இதற்குத் தலைவரா யிருந்த சிற்றரசருள்ளே எழினியும் பிட்டங் கொற்றனும் புறநானூற்றிற் பாடப்பட்டோர்.

இங்ஙனம் வருமேதுக்களால் தமிழ்ச்சங்கப் புலவருள்ளே ஒரு சிலர் ஈழநாட்டுப் புலவ ராதல் வேண்டும் மெனவும், தமிழ்ச் சங்கப்புலவராற் பாடப்பட்டாருள்ளும் ஒரு சிலர் ஈழநாட்டா ராதல் வேண்டுமெனவும் அவரே ஈழநாட்டிலே முதலில் தமிழ் வளர்த்தா ராதல் வேண்டுமெனவும் அநுமிக்க இடமாகின்றது.

APPENDIX.

PANDIYAN COINS

BY

DIWAN BAHADUR T. DESIKACHARI B.A., B.L., M.R.A.S.

NOTE.

The plates appended to the list of the Pandiyan and Chola Coins have been prepared from photographs of plaster casts of selected specimens from the best known collection of South Indian Coins. Most of them are from the cabinet of myself and Diwan Bahadur T. M. Rangachariar, Retired District Judge. My obligations are however due to the courtesy of Mr. Thurston, late Superintendent of the Government Central Museum, who had permitted to me catalogue the Museum Pandiya and Chola Coins, as well as to the Rev. Dr. Tracy and to Mr. C. Rajagopalachariar pleader, Tindivanam, who had placed at my disposal their valuable specimens of Pandiyan and Chola Coins to enable me to prepare an up-to-date list of the issues of the two great Dravidian Powers, who more than any other Kingdom of the south represented the ancient civilisation, art and commerce of South India.

For the photographs from which the plates were prepared I am indebted to the kindness of Rao Bahadur T. Sundara Rao, C.I.S.O., whose invaluable assistance to me in the preparation of the plaster casts I gratefully acknowledge.

T. D.

LIST OF PANDIYAN COINS.

PLATE I.

Fig. 1 A. E. *Obverse* :—Elephant facing the right, with a *Chaitya* in front.

Reverse :—A triangular diagram, with a wavy line above.

Fig. 2 A. E. *Obverse* :—Elephant facing the right, ridden by a warrior or a king with the mahout in front.

Reverse :—Same as fig. 1.

Fig. 3 A. E. *Obverse* :—Elephant facing the right with riders as in fig. 2 and two standing figures in front of the elephant.

Reverse :—Same as fig. 1.

Fig. 4 A. E. *Obverse* :—Elephant facing the right with riders and standing human figures as in fig. 3 together with a well executed *chakram* (the sacred wheel), in the field above the standing figure.

Reverse :—Same as fig. 1.

Fig. 5 A. E. *Obverse* :—Same as fig. 3 with Buddhist symbols above the elephant.

Reverse :—Same as fig. 1.

Fig. 6 A. E. *Obverse* :—Elephant and with the *chakram* (the sacred wheel) and the *kumbham* (the sacred pot) above.

Reverse :—Same as fig. 1.

Fig. 7 A. E. *Obverse* :—The sacred tree of the Buddhists and other emblems.

Reverse :—Same as fig. 1.

Fig. 8 A. E. *Obverse* :—Bull advancing to the right, with the sacred tree in front and the sun and moon above.

Reverse :—Same as fig. 1.

Fig. 9 A. E. *Obverse* :—Bull advancing to the right, with the crescent in the field above.

Reverse :—Same as fig. 1.

Fig. 10 A. E. *Obverse* :—Bull advancing to the right.

Reverse :—Same as fig. 1.

Fig. 11 A. E. *Obverse* :—Bull passant with the sacred tree in front.

Reverse :—Same as fig. 1.

Fig. 12 A. E. *Obverse* :—The Buddhist symbols, the *chakram*, *chaitya* and the elephant.

Reverse :—Same as fig. 1.

Fig. 13 A. E. *Obverse* :—Single fish in a perpendicular position with a lamp or standard by its side.

Reverse :—Defaced.

Fig. 14 A. E. *Obverse* :—Three fishes, with the crescent above.

Reverse :—Recumbent bull with the crescent above.

Fig. 15 A. E. *Obverse* :—Recumbent bull with the *trisul* in front and the crescent above.

Reverse :—Two fishes flanked by sacrificial lamps.

Fig. 16 A. E. *Obverse* :—Two fishes separated by a tall standard or umbrella.

Reverse :—Recumbent bull, right, with the crescent above.

Fig. 17 A. E. *Obverse*:—Maneless lion passant to the left with two fishes separated by a sceptre above.

Reverse:—Standing figure of a King in his regal robes, (as in fig. 46) which is the characteristic feature of the reverse of the coins of the Sinhalese Kings of Ceylon.

Fig. 18 A. E. *Obverse*:—A seated figure with that of a fish to its left.

Reverse:—Same as in fig. 17.

Fig. 19 A. E. *Obverse*:—Single fish between the sun and the crescent moon.

Reverse:—Same as in fig. 17.

Fig. 20 A. E. *Obverse*:—Seated figure with two fishes to its left.

Reverse:—Same as in fig. 17.

Fig. 21 A. E. *Obverse and Reverse*:—Same as fig. 20 but of a different type.

PLATE II.

Fig. 22 A. E. *Obverse*:—Two fishes separated by a sceptre with the crescent above.

Reverse:—The Tamil legend: கோதண்டராமன் (Kōdaṇḍarāman) with the state umbrella flanked by flags.

Fig. 23 A. E. *Obverse*:—The *vishnupâda* (feet of Vishnu) with the 'chank' (conch shell) to the left of the central device and the state umbrella flanked by flags above.

Reverse:—Below the state umbrella flanked by flags is the Tamil legend கலியுகராமன் (Kaliyugarāman).

Fig. 24 A. E. Variant of fig. 23.

Fig. 25 A. E. *Obverse* :—Standing figure in regal robes with two fishes separated by a sceptre to its right.

Reverse :—Seated figure with legend to its left ஜெகவீர (Jagavira.)

Fig. 26 A. E. *Obverse* :—Standing figure facing the left, with two fishes separated by a sceptre to the left of the standing figure ; the whole surrounded by a ring of dots.

Reverse .—Seated figure facing the left with the Tamil legend ஜெகவீர (Jagavira.)

Fig. 27 A. E. *Obverse* :—Variant of fig. 25. Standing figure with a lamp to its left.

Reverse :—Seated figure with legend in Tamil to its left பூதலவி (Butalavi.)

Fig. 28 A. E. *Obverse* :—Standing figure with a lamp to its left.

Reverse :—Seated figure with Tamil legend சேர குலராமன் (Chērakularāman.)

Fig. 29 A. E. *Obverse* :—Standing figure in regal robes, as in fig. 46.

Reverse :—Tamil legend சோணாடுகொண்டான் 'Cho-nadukondan' or 'Cheranadukondan'.

Fig. 30 A. E. *Observe* :—Standing figure in regal robes, as in fig. 46.

Reverse :—Seated figure of King with Tamil legend to its left பூதல (Butala) and two fishes below the legend.

Fig. 31 A. E. *Obverse* :—Standing figure in regal robes, as in fig. 46.

Reverse :—Seated figure of King with Tamil legend to its left பூதல (*Butala.*)

Fig. 32 A. E. *Observe* :—Single fish flanked by lamps or standards with the state umbrella above.

Reverse :—Tamil legend அவனிபேந்திரன் (Avanl-pēndiran) with the state umbrella flanked by flags above.

Figs. 33 & 33 *a* A.E.:—Fig. 33 *a Obverse:* A tree on a pedastal with a bull below.

Fig. 33. *Reverse*:—Tamil legend அவனிபேந்திரன் (?) (Avanipendiran?).

Fig. 34 A. E. *Obverse*:—Standing figure in regal robes, as in fig. 46.

Reverse:—Tamil legend எல்லந்தலை (Ellanthalai.)

Fig. 35 A. E. *Obverse*:—Standing figure in regal robes, as in fig. 46.

Reverse:—Single fish flanked by lamps or standards with the Tamil legend around எல்லாந்தலையானன் (Ellāntalaiyānān)

Fig. 36 A. E. *Obverse*:—Standing figure as in fig. 35.

Reverse:—The Tamil legend எல்லாந்தலையான[illegible] (Ellāntalaiyānān) between two fishes.

Fig. 37 A. E. *Obverse*:—Standing figure as in fig. 46.

Reverse:—The same legend as in 35 surrounding two fishes in the centre.

Fig. 38 Variant of fig. 36.

Fig. 39, „ 40, „ 41, „ 42, „ 43 } Two fishes crossed, with the following emblems appearing in a different order in each different issue in the angles formed by the intersection of the fishes:—the *chank*, the sceptre, the trident, the crescent, and the Tamil syllable சு (su.)

Fig. 43*a*. The Tamil legend கச்சிவழங்கும்பெருமாள் (Kacchivalangumperumāḷ.) This is the legend on the reverse of all the figures Nos. 39 to 43.

Fig. 44 A. E. *Obverse*:—Two fishes crosed below the crescent moon, with doubtful emblems in the angles.

Reverse:—கனிய. வி. பெ.

Fig. 45 A. E. *Obverse* :—Two fishes crossed, below the crescent moon, with stars in the field to the left of the principal device.

Reverse :—Below the state umbrella, flanked by *chowries* or flags, is the Tamil legend similar to that in fig. 44.

PLATE III.

Fig. 46 A. E. *Obverse* :—Standing figure of King in regal robes

Reverse :—Two fishes separated by a sceptre and flanked by lamps or standards, with the Tamil legend வீரபாண்டியன் (Vīra Pāṇḍiyan.)

Fig. 47 A. E. *Obverse* :—Same as in fig. 46.

Reverse :—Same reverse as fig. 46, but of a different type.

Fig. 48 A. E. *Obverse* :—Same as No. 46.

Reverse :—Two fishes separated by a sceptre and flanked by lamps with Tamil legend above வீரபா—(Vīra pā.)

Fig. 49 A. E. *Obverse* :—Standing figure of King in legal robes.

Reverse :—Above two fishes separated by a crook or a sceptre, the the Tamil legend குலசேகரன் (Kulasēkaran.)

Fig.49*a* A. E. *Obverse* :—Elephant passant to the left, with emblems or characters above, which cannot be deciphered.

Reverse :—Above two fishes separated by a sceptre is the Tamil legend குலசேகரன் (Kulasekaran.)

Figs. 50 & 51 A. E. *Obverse* :—Standing figure with hands joined as in the act of worship with the legend in Tamil distributed on either side of the figure: சுந்தர பாண்டியன்.

Reverse:—Two fishes separated by a sceptre: above this device in the state umbrella flanked by flags.

Fig. 52 A. E. *Obverse:*—Standing figure of King arrayed in regal robes.

Reverse:—Seated figure similarly clad with legend in Tamil to its left: சுந்த: (Sunda.)

Figs. 53, 54*a* & 55 A. E. *Obverse:*—Two fishes separated by a sceptre with the crescent above as in fig. 54.

Reverse:—Tamil legend சுந்தரபாண்டியன்(Sundara Pandyan) as in figs. 53 54*a* and 55.

Figs. 56 & 57 & 64 A.E. *Obverse:*—Standing figure of king clad in regal robes, as in 56 and 64.

Reverse:—Tamil legend சுந்தரபாண்டியன் (Sundara Pandyan) as in 56, 57 and 64.

Fig. 58 A. E. *Obverse:*—Boar facing the right on a pedestal with the sun and the crescent moon above.

Fig. 59 *Reverse* of fig. 58:—Two fishes separated by a sceptre with legend in Tamil சுந்தர பாண்டியன் (Sundara Pandyan).

Fig. 60 A. E. Same *Obverse* and *Reverse* as in fig. 56.

Fig. 61 & 62A.E. *Obverse:*—Two fishes separated by an umbrella, as in 61.

Reverse:—Tamil legend...., வேமபெருமாள் (Vemaperumal), as in 61 *a* and 62.

Fig. 63 A. E. *Obverse:*—Single fish flanked by lamps or standards with the state umbrella above.

Reverse:—Below the state umbrella flanked by flags is the Tamil legend அவனிபேந் திரன் (Avanipēndiran.)

Fig. 65 66 A. E. *Obverse:*— Two fishes in a perpendicular position. (Fig. 65.)

Reverse :—Tamil legend ஸ்ரீஅவனிபசேகரகோளகன் (Sri Avanipa Sekara Kolaka) (fig. 66) c o figs. 32 to 33*a*.

PLATE IV.

Fig. 67 A. E. *Obverse* :—Seated figure with single fish to its left.

Reverse :—Tamil legend வீரபா (Vīrapa ?)

Fig. 68 A. E. *Obverse* :—Two fishes separated by a sceptre.

Reverse :—Tamil legend.

Fig. 69 & 70 A. E. *Obverse* :—Standing figure of King.

Reverse :—Two fishes separated by a dagger with Tamil legend விஸ்வநாதன் (Visvanādan).

Fig. 71 A. E. *Obverse* :—Standing Ceylon figure.

Reverse :—Below the state umbrella flanked by *chowries*, is the Tamil legend :— குலசேகரன்.

Fig. 72 A. E. *Obverse* :—Standing Ceylon figure.

Reverse :—Two fishes separated by a sceptre.

Fig. 73 A. E. *Obverse* :—The anthropoid kite (*garuda*) with wings extended, and bearing the *chank* and *chukra*.(conch and discus.)

Reverse :—The Tamil legend சமரகோலாகலன் (Samarakōlākalan.) as in Fig. 74.

Fig. 74 A. E. *Obverse* :—The anthropoid kite as in fig. 73, above a fish.

Reverse :—The Tamil legend ச ம ர கோ லா க ல ன் (Samarakōlākalan.)

Fig. 75 A. E. *Overse* :—The anthropoid kite as in fig. 73.

Reverse :—Tamil beyond ச ம ர கோ லா க ல ன் (Samarakōlākalan.)

Fig. 76 A. E. *Obverse* :—The anthropoid kite.

Reverse :—Two fishes separated by sceptre.

Fig. 77 A. E. *Obverse* :—Bull passant facing the left with a dagger in front.

Reverse :—Tamil legend கோனேரி (ராயன்?)

Fig. 78 A. E. *Obverse* :—Bull passant to the left, bearing the state umbrella.

Reverse :—The Tamil legend கோனேரிராயன் a dagger separating the legend.

Fig. 79 A. E. *Obverse* :—The anthropoid kite beneath an ornamented canopy.

Reverse :—Tamil legend புவனேகவீரன். (Buvanēkavīran.)

Fig. 80 A. E. *Obverse* :—The anthropoid kite.

Reverse :—Tamil legend : புவனேகவீரன்.

Fig. 81 A. E. *Obverse* :—Dancing figure.

Reverse :—Tamil legend மதுரை, (Madurai.)

Fig. 82 A. E. *Obverse* —Recumbent bull on a pedestal, facing the left.

Reverse :—In a rectangular enclosure subdivided in four sections is the Telugu legend (Mangama.)

Fig. 83 A. E. *Obverse* :—Recumbant bull to the left.

Reverse :—Tamil legend பழனி (Palani.)

Fig. 83aA.E. *Obverse* :—A dagger.

Reverse :—Single fish surrounded by the Tamil legend : பழனி (Palani.)

Fig. 84 A. E. *Obverse* :—A rectangular diagram in the form of a cross.

Reverse :—Single fish, with legend: பழனி (Palani.)

Fig. 85 A. E. *Obverse* :—Horse passant to the right.

Reverse :—Tamil legend பழனி (Palani.)

Fig. 86 A. E. *Obverse* :—Horse passant to the right.

Reverse —Tamil legend விருபாசி (Virupachi.)

Fig. 87 A. E. *Obverse* :—Tamil legend : மதுரை (Madurai.)

Reverse :—Telugu legend...........(Madura.)

PLATE I

PLATE II

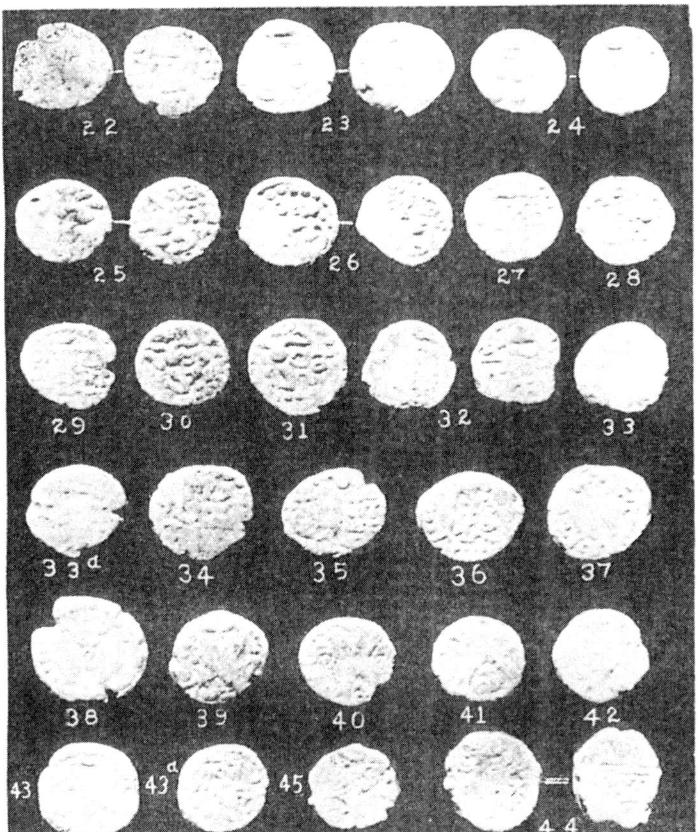
22
23
24
25
26
27
28
29
30
31
32
33
33a
34
35
36
37
38
39
40
41
42
43
43a
45
44

PLATE III

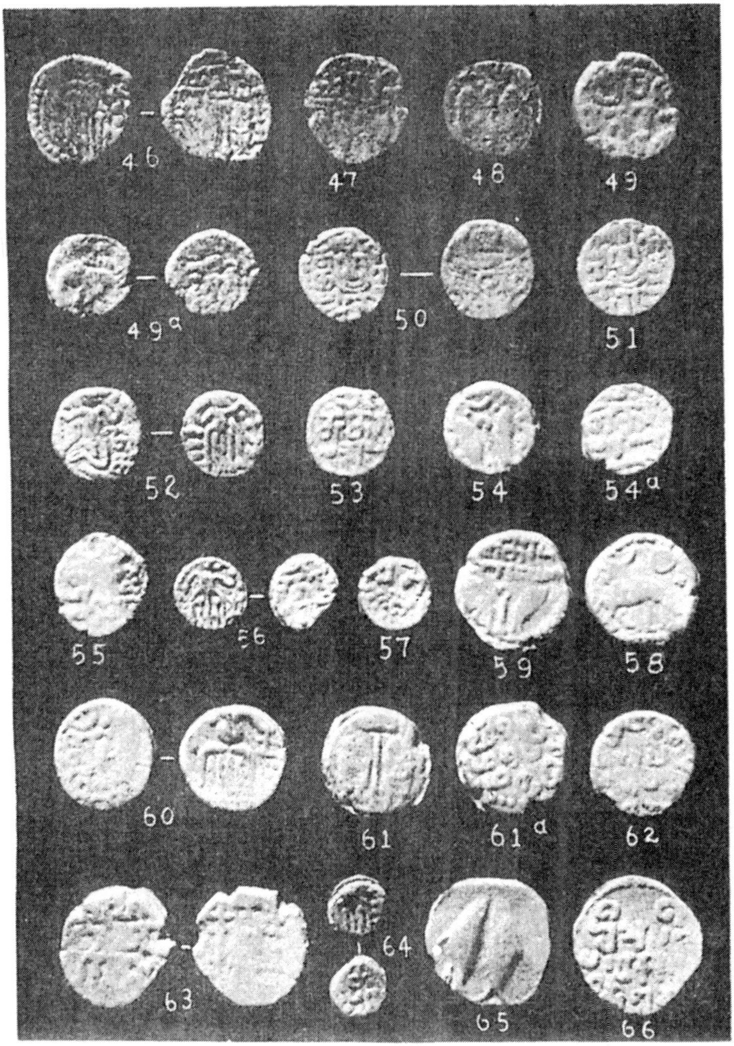
46
47
48
49
49a
50
51
52
53
54
54a
55
56
57
59
58
60
61
61a
62
63
64
65
66

PLATE IV